"Joseph Louis Bernardin was simply one of the preeminent bishops of the past century. He achieved that privileged status through his always prudent and authentic understanding and pursuit of the Church's tradition and her potential. While he enjoyed the confidence of the USA Bishops because of repeated situations in the post-Conciliar era wherein he displayed an extraordinary capacity to bring respected consensus to difficult circumstances, he eventually suffered at the hands of those who chose to pursue an ecclesial vision of intransigence and reaction. I consider myself a fortunate man to have witnessed his faith and pastoral style firsthand and to have learned most of all from his example. He never lost the common touch and this made him both an approachable pastor and a credible church guide. There are few bishops today who might be considered his equal in wisdom or genius. This new biography gives us an excellent perspective on how this extraordinary man of faith and pastoral skill developed those virtues throughout his life. It will only add to his stature and hopefully confirm our respect for this extraordinary shepherd of souls."

> —Archbishop Wilton D. Gregory
> Archdiocese of Atlanta

"Joseph Bernardin was one of the most influential Catholic leaders of the second half of the twentieth century. His pastoral, administrative, and teaching ability was clearly evident as he served the Church through some extraordinary times. In this book, Steven Millies informs us of the many issues of Church life and societal complexities the Cardinal addressed and impacted through his forty-four years as a priest and thirty years as a bishop. He was truly a man of peace. From my own perspective, Steven captured well the persona of this wise and gentle leader beloved by so, so many."

> —Monsignor Kenneth Velo
> DePaul University

People of God

Remarkable Lives, Heroes of Faith

People of God is a series of inspiring biographies for the general reader. Each volume offers a compelling and honest narrative of the life of an important twentieth- or twenty-first-century Catholic. Some living and some now deceased, each of these women and men has known challenges and weaknesses familiar to most of us but responded to them in ways that call us to our own forms of heroism. Each offers a credible and concrete witness of faith, hope, and love to people of our own day.

More titles to follow. . . .

Joseph Bernardin

Seeking Common Ground

Steven P. Millies

LITURGICAL PRESS
Collegeville, Minnesota

www.litpress.org

Cover design by Stefan Killen Design. Cover illustration by Philip Bannister.

1   2   3   4   5   6   7   8   9

Library of Congress Control Number: 2016931690

ISBN 978-0-8146-4806-3   978-0-8146-4831-5 (ebook)

Dedicated to the ministries of
Francis,
Bishop of Rome

Blase Cupich,
Archbishop of Chicago

Peter Clarke,
Priest of Charleston

Contents

Acknowledgements

The pleasure of writing about Cardinal Bernardin has been meeting so many people who want to talk about him. It has been my privilege for the last several months to find Joseph Bernardin alive in conversation with the people who knew and loved him. This book would not exist without the help of those people.

First, I have to thank Fr. Peter Clarke. Peter is a good friend and a longtime priest of the Diocese of Charleston. Peter knew "Joe" while he was in the Charleston diocese, and he invited me into a circle of friends on the University of South Carolina's Bernardin Endowment Committee. That committee, of which I am now a member, has sponsored a Bernardin Lecture every year since the cardinal's death and is raising funds toward a Joseph Cardinal Bernardin Chair in Moral, Ethical, and Religious Studies. Fellow committee members include Libby Bernardin and Fr. Scott Donahue, both of whom have been generous enough to share their recollections about Cardinal Bernardin with me. They also brought me into contact with some other wonderful people.

I also must thank Archbishop Wilton Gregory of Atlanta for spending some time with me to talk about the cardinal, as well as Msgr. John Canary, Msgr. Ken Velo, and Fr. Michael Place from the Archdiocese of Chicago. Pastor Sam Miglarese of First Presbyterian Church of Durham and Duke University generously shared some of his personal mementos and his time with me. He and I met in the home of his mother, Louise, at the table where Fr. Bernardin sometimes used to come have Sunday breakfast after Mass. They both helped me understand Cardinal Bernardin's life better. The cardinal's cousin, Anita Orf, provided some of her memories about the Bernardin family. Rev. Mark Francis, CSV, president of the Catholic Theological Union, and Sheila McLaughlin, the director of CTU's Bernardin Center, also were very generous to share their time and resources with me. Father Al Spilly not only gave an enlightening interview about the cardinal, but provided gracious hospitality at his new home in the Archdiocese of San Antonio. Father Louis J. Cameli of the Archdiocese of Chicago was kind to spend a morning recalling the cardinal with me, and Fr. Richard Rohr found moments in his busy schedule to recall fondly his "Cardinal Protector." I was pleased to meet an Aiken neighbor, Joan McGinty, who once worked for Archbishop Paul Hallinan and spent an afternoon talking to me about that marvelous shepherd, and Fr. Thomas Nolker spoke to me about his time as Archbishop Bernardin's assistant in Cincinnati.

No project like this one can succeed without the support of the under-recognized professionals who manage the historical memory of the church in diocesan and archdiocesan archives. I am most grateful to the staffs in Charleston, Atlanta, Cincinnati, and Chicago, and I must single out for special thanks Brian Fahey of the Charleston archive, Angelique Richardson of Atlanta, Richard Hamilton of Cincinnati, and Meg Hall of Chicago. I also must extend a special word of thanks to Sister Sandra Makowsi, SSMN, the chancellor of the Diocese of Charleston, and Kevin J. Marzalik, the former chancellor of the Archdiocese of Chicago, who both waived some of the restrictions on Cardinal Bernardin materials that enriched this project.

Special thanks go to Chuck Lamphier who works in the office of Mission Engagement and Church Affairs at the University of Notre Dame and, more importantly, is a good friend of many years. Chuck spent some of his valuable time tracking down sources for this book and almost as much time listening to me talk about it.

I owe a great debt to both Barry Hudock and Andy Edwards at Liturgical Press. They gave me the opportunity to write this book, which I have enjoyed so much. And, they provided no small amount of help bringing it to readers.

Research for this project was sustained by a generous grant from the University of South Carolina Aiken and Dr. Jeff Priest, executive vice chancellor for Academic Affairs. Dr. David Dillard-Wright, the chair of the Department of History, Political Science, and Philosophy, also provided essential support.

Thanks always go to my parents, Diane and Paul Millies, and to my wife's parents, Aileen and Joe Giannelli, for their constant love and support.

But the final thanks go to my family. My wife, Mary Claire, listened patiently while I talked about this project, and she provided crackerjack copyediting at the end. She, with our children Andrew and Nora, made the greatest sacrifices to see this project to completion.

Steven P. Millies
Aiken, South Carolina
August 25, 2015
*Feasts of Saint Joseph of Calasanz
and Saint Louis of France*

Note on Sources

Most of Cardinal Bernardin's papers are housed at the Archdiocese of Chicago's Joseph Cardinal Bernardin Archives and Records Center. The archdiocese's archival policies dictate that an archbishop's papers shall not be available for researchers until twenty-five years after his death. For this reason, the Bernardin papers were not fully processed at the time when I viewed them. This creates a dilemma when I cite to these sources, since the organization of the documents is quite likely to be different after 2021.

The "Addresses and Talks" collection most probably will be unaffected by future processing. They are in a digital database, a really marvelous resource. Many of the collections that are cited throughout this book almost certainly will be affected. In consultation with the archival staff, I have elected to identify those collections by these names:

Joseph Cardinal Bernardin Subject Files
Joseph Cardinal Bernardin Speeches and Talks
Office of Divine Worship Series Papal Visit (1987) Series
"Our Communion, Our Peace, Our Promise" Series
School Closings Series (1990)
"The Family Gathered Here Before You" Series

I encourage future researchers to bear in mind some of my citations' transitory condition, even as I hope this book enriches their future work.

Abbreviations

In citing works in the notes, short titles generally have been used. Works frequently cited have been identified by the following abbreviations:

BJB   Bishop Joseph L. Bernardin Collection. Archdiocese of Atlanta Office of Archives and Records.

CCC   Administration of Cemeteries 1952–1959 Collection. Diocese of Charleston Archives.

JCD   John Cardinal Dearden Collection. Archdiocese of Detroit Archives.

JLB   Joseph Cardinal Bernardin Collection. Archdiocese of Chicago Joseph Cardinal Bernardin Archives and Records Center.

NCCB NCCB Collection. American Catholic History Research Center.

PJH   Archbishop Paul J. Hallinan Collection. Archdiocese of Atlanta Office of Archives and Records.

PSF   Priest Subject Files. Diocese of Charleston Archives.

SW1   Alphonse P. Spilly, CPPS, ed., *Selected Works of Joseph Cardinal Bernardin, Volume One: Homilies and Teaching Documents* (Collegeville, MN: Liturgical Press, 2000).

SW2   Alphonse P. Spilly, CPPS, ed., *Selected Works of Joseph Cardinal Bernardin, Volume Two: Church and Society* (Collegeville, MN: Liturgical Press, 2000).

WCB   Diocese of Charleston Archives, Fr. William C. Burns Subject Files.

Introduction

Cardinal Joseph Bernardin carried a copy of the Prayer of Saint Francis with him in his pocket. Sometimes he referred to the prayer in his speeches or homilies. At a particularly difficult meeting, when he knew people were going to be tense and the stakes were high, he would pull the text out of his pocket and offer it as an opening prayer. Surely, he had no need to read the prayer from a card. He must have known it by heart:

> Lord, make me an instrument of your peace. Where there is hatred, let me sow love; where there is injury, pardon; where there is doubt, faith; where there is despair, hope; where there is darkness, light; where there is sadness, joy. O, Divine Master, grant that I may not so much seek to be consoled as to console; to be understood as to understand; to be loved as to love. For it is in giving that we receive; it is in pardoning that we are pardoned; it is in dying that we are born again to eternal life.

Yet, these familiar words of reconciliation were worth getting exactly right. There were two things about Joseph Bernardin that everyone around him knew they could depend on. He wanted to reconcile people, and his precise personality wanted everything to be done just right.

The influence of Franciscan spirituality on Joseph Bernardin at first may be surprising. So far as any part of his well-documented public life tells us, he had no particularly obvious Franciscan connection. But Joseph did feel a deep connection to St. Francis throughout his life. First, Joseph was the son of Italian immigrants. Throughout his life, that heritage remained important to him, and it shaped his spiritual life. It is not surprising that Joseph felt close to the poor man of Assisi, who lived and died just down the Adriatic coast from his ancestral home in the mountains of northern Italy. Then there is Joseph's lifelong devotion to peacemaking. Joseph Bernardin spent his lifetime bringing people together over their differences, succeeding more often than not because of his always thorough preparation and the genuine respect he showed to everyone. Finally, Joseph's lifetime in the church was one spent on much the same mission given to Francis: "Go and repair my house." As St. Francis had reformed the church of the thirteenth century, Joseph's ministry was absorbed by realizing the potential in the reforms of the Second Vatican Council. Joseph was a devoted churchman. He loved the church. More than anything, he wanted the church to be even more relevant to the world we live in and to address more directly the joys and the hopes, the griefs, and the sorrows of the men and women of today. No mission could have meant more to him than to play his role in making that happen.

Monsignor Ken Velo, in the well-remembered homily at Cardinal Bernardin's funeral, asked the questions over and over: Didn't he teach us? Didn't he show us the way? The answers to those questions only can be found in an examination of his life.

CHAPTER ONE

An Immigrant Family (1928–66)

Joseph Louis Bernardin was born in South Carolina—and he arrived there only a short time after his parents.

Giuseppe Bernardin, his father, was a stonecutter and the second-youngest of six brothers who came to the United States between 1907 and 1920 to seek their fortunes.[1] These sons of Maddalena and Gaspare Bernardin all left their home in Tonadico di Primiero, a tiny hamlet fixed in the heart of the Dolomites and, at that time, a part of the Austro-Hungarian Empire. It was there that they learned the stonecutter's trade, against the backdrop of those dramatic, limestone peaks that surrounded their home. Antonio, Giovanni, and Gaspare were the three eldest, and they came first to Barre, Vermont, in 1907. Barre had been attracting stonecutters throughout the nineteenth century, having proclaimed itself the "Granite Capital of the World." But by 1920, the Bernardins had relocated to South Carolina where rich deposits of blue granite and a need for skilled craftsmen to work the stone made a more attractive opportunity.

Giacomo followed his brothers to America in 1914, then Giuseppe in 1919, and Severino in 1920.

None of these brothers planned to stay in America. Instead, they hoped to make their fortunes and return home. But first came the Depression, then World War II, and by 1945 their families had become so well established that there seemed to be no reason to leave. Indeed, visiting home shortly after the war ended, the Bernardins all felt certain they were better off in America than in war-ravaged Europe.[2] The Bernardins would be Americans after all.

Giuseppe was twenty-nine when he came to the United States, moving into a crowded home with his brothers Giovanni, Gaspare, and Giacomo, and their families. (By 1920 Antonio was living at a different address in Columbia.) At one time or another, all of these brothers worked as stonecutters for the Columbia Granite Company, where Giovanni had risen to manager. Immigration records do not confirm precisely when Giuseppe and his younger brother, Severino, returned to Italy for a visit in the mid- to late-1920s, but both spent their time back in Tonadico courting two sisters—Maria Simion and Lina Simion. Giuseppe returned to the United States on September 21, 1927, with his new bride Maria. The marriage had been celebrated in Italy, and Maria already was pregnant when she arrived in the United States. Joseph Louis would be born just seven months later, practically an immigrant himself.

A dark cloud hung over this happy story of immigrant striving and new marriage. Giuseppe already had suffered from cancer before he met Maria. He had cancerous tumors surgically removed before he emigrated to the United States, but he seemed healthy and fully recovered when he became Maria's suitor. Even so, he insisted that Maria be fully informed by his doctors in Tonadico about his health problems before he would hear her agree to marry him. Maria was undeterred, and the marriage went off shortly thereafter. The couple set off for their new home in America looking forward to a happy and prosperous life together. Perhaps even that early, they knew that they already had begun a family.

Joseph Bernardin was only six years old when his father died in 1934. The cancer returned in the form of sarcoma, a malignant growth of the soft tissues such as cartilage, fat, or muscle. Giuseppe's physician recorded on his death certificate that he suffered from sarcomas on his shoulder, neck, and head. We also know from Joseph's recollection that doctors tried to remove the tumors once they recurred. In his spiritual memoir, *The Gift of Peace*, Joseph remembered a time when he was very young. Young Joseph had fallen. He had not hurt himself but was frightened in that way that a sudden shock will make small children cry. Giuseppe had just had surgery to treat a tumor in his left shoulder, but Joseph describes a clear memory of his father racing to him, picking him up, and cradling him. From his father's arms, young Joseph could see the blood soak through Giuseppe's bandages and shirt from the exertion. "He paid no attention to himself," Joseph recalled, and "all he wanted was to be sure I was all right.[3] The truth is that the historical record does not tell us very much more about Giuseppe Bernardin. Like so many immigrants who came to the United States looking for their fortunes, his legacy is less found in the details of his daily life or what he thought about the problems of his time than it is with the children, grandchildren, and great grandchildren he left behind. Much like the raw granite he shaped as a stonecutter, his descendants bear the imprint of his work, his care, his personality, and the love with which he devoted himself to them. In one sense we cannot really know Giuseppe from where we are today. There is no record of his life to match the record of his son's life. But in a greater sense, though he was only six years old when Giuseppe died, we do know him through Joseph and the Bernardin family. There is no doubt Joseph was aware of that, too.

After Giuseppe's death, life was hard for Maria and her children. Joseph's sister Elaine was born just months before Giuseppe died. Once the family patriarch was gone, Maria and her two children were left to face life in the Depression. But they were not left alone. They had each other, of course. They also had uncles, aunts, and cousins—all of the members of the growing Bernardin family living in the United States. And, of course, Maria had her sister Lina who had married Giuseppe's brother Severino. After Giuseppe's death, the two families lived together for a time. Giuseppe's children, Joseph and Elaine, grew up together with Lina and Severino's children, John and Anita. In that home Joseph knew the closeness of family perhaps better than he might otherwise have known it because of his father's death. That closeness would remain throughout Joseph's life. He never would lose the ties of intimacy with his Bernardin family. Looking back, Joseph remembered that "the Bernardin family is known to be a very gentle, reconciling influence. I didn't know my father well, but my uncles and the other members of my family who still reside in Italy are peaceful, calm people who always tried to see good in others and tried to reconcile differences."[4]

In the years that followed, cousin John Bernardin's wife, Libby, would echo that description to describe Joseph and his family this way: "He had a wonderfully quiet, gentle way. And patience, that's another Bernardin trait. They are patient, understanding and loving men . . . the most wonderful men I've ever met."[5] Joseph's friend and biographer,

Eugene Kennedy, credited Joseph's Italian Mediterranean heritage for those gentle qualities of personality that Libby ascribed to all of the Bernardins and which figured so prominently in Joseph's public ministry. But one last note may be worth making about the Bernardin family heritage and how much it was visible in Joseph's life and ministry. Tonadico di Primiero is not simply another Italian hamlet. The Trento region in northern Italy, where Tonadico is located, sits at a European crossroads. Lying only a two-hour drive from the present-day Austrian border and a three-hour drive from the Slovenian border, the history of this region does not permit us simply to say it is Italian.

When most of the Bernardin brothers left Tonadico, Trento still was part of the Austro-Hungarian Empire. Joseph's uncle Giovanni Bernardin reported on census forms and ship manifests between 1923 and 1957 that his ethnicity was German, and Giacomo Bernardin's 1914 record of entry into the United States reports him to have been Magyar. There is no doubt that the Bernardins were ethnically Italian: Joseph and his family spoke Italian, cooked Italian foods, and identified as Italian. But those records about Giovanni and Giacomo help us to understand the complexity of life in the Dolomites. At least three distinct linguistic and cultural groups live there today side by side: Italian, German, and Ladin. It is not uncommon in this region for each town to have a widely recognized German name to accompany its Italian name. (Tonadico also is known as Thunadlich.) These cultures have learned to live together through the centuries, regardless of the political winds that have blown the borders in different directions. German speakers are free to speak German, Italians to speak Italian, and even the Ladin minority can find its heritage represented on the trilingual traffic signs. The gentleness, patience, and willingness to tolerate other points of view that Libby Bernardin saw among the Bernardin men—and which the world saw in Joseph's ministry—must have owed something to the climate of a part of Europe, more Alpine than Mediterranean, where so many different people had learned to get along.

The ability to get along probably served young Joseph Bernardin well as an Italian and a Catholic in South Carolina only seventy years after the conclusion of the Civil War. The narrative of the South's noble, lost cause already had hardened a sense of southern identity not just against the North but also against all outsiders. At the end of a period in the late-nineteenth and early-twentieth centuries that saw tens of millions of immigrants flood into the United States, the 1930 census found that South Carolina was home to the lowest number of persons with foreign parents (6,477— about 0.3 percent of the population) in the nation, with North Carolina and Georgia not far ahead. The same census found that South Carolina was home to only 188 persons born in Italy, and records show that less than 1 percent of the state's population was Catholic at that time. Looking back on those years, however, Joseph would recall that "we experienced ecumenism in Columbia then at the practical and personal level long before people in other parts of the country."[6] Surrounded by Protestants, in a southern culture that must have regarded them as outsiders, the Bernardins learned to live with other people just as the Italians had learned to live alongside the Germans in Tonadico. Joseph hardly was alone to look back fondly on the opportunities he had growing up in such diverse circumstances, perhaps sometimes seeing the world from the perspective of an outsider. In 1983 Joseph's sister Elaine looked back to say that "I'm satisfied we were much better off than [if we had grown up] in a big city neighborhood with nothing but other

Italian Catholics."[7] Her brother agreed, and "said he was never aware of feeling any prejudice as a Roman Catholic."[8] Through his father's illness and death, in the strange way that it happens sometimes in life, this perspective on a different, more diverse world outside the comfort of an Italian Catholic enclave opened for Joseph. Of course, without the gentle influence of his father and his family, young Joseph would not have been a person who recognized the opportunity that different perspective gave him.

But personality and natural dispositions count for something, too. Every available report tells us that Joseph was a serious and thoughtful boy. His aunt, Lina Simion Bernardin, recalled that "I never had to spank him."[9] His sister recalled that Joseph was "well-rounded," and, "He worked at odd jobs around the house and in the neighborhood. He had a lot of friends and he had time to spend with everyone, young and old."[10] Perhaps it could not have been otherwise. To have lost a father and find his mother depending on him when he was only six years old must have had an impact on young Joseph. Eugene Kennedy wrote, "Joseph learned as he grew up that hardship was not softened by escape," and "this bred a deep, spiritual sense into Joseph Bernardin's bones, I understood after we became friends."[11] Little surprise, then, that Joseph began to nurture a vocation to the priesthood while he was a young man. Much later, his executive assistant in Chicago, Monsignor Ken Velo, would remember the influence of priests Joseph knew in Columbia as a young man.[12] Eugene Kennedy named, in particular Fr. Charles Sheedy and Msgr. Martin Murphy as priests Joseph had remembered to him.[13] But Joseph, himself, was careful to give credit also to "The Sisters of Charity who run the hospital [Providence Hospital in Columbia]—Sister Mary Julia in particular" for encouraging him to consider the religious life.[14]

Joseph's path to the priesthood was not an easy one. Graduating from Columbia High School in 1944, he earned a scholarship to the University of South Carolina and decided to enter the premed program. Perhaps it is not surprising that a young man who saw doctors and nurses tend to his ailing father, who came to know the sisters at Providence Hospital so well, thought about becoming a doctor. But as Joseph told the story, two priests he knew helped him to understand that his desire to become a physician signaled a desire to serve others. Those priests nurtured the idea that Joseph could follow through on that desire and help people even more meaningfully if he became a priest. It was one thing for Joseph to come to that understanding; helping his mother to understand that was quite a different thing.

Maria was like a lot of immigrant parents who came to the United States and wanted a better life for their children. As Maria regarded her only son: "Becoming a doctor was a pathway up; becoming a priest was a continuing commitment to poverty."[15] One family member recalled "a tense scene on the steps of St. Peter's Church where Maria Bernardin bawled out Msgr. Murphy for having an undue influence on Joe's decision" to pursue the priesthood.[16] Maria had not changed her mind even after young Joseph had a successful interview with Charleston Bishop Edmund Walsh for admission to the priesthood. A few days after that interview, Joseph wrote to the bishop saying, "My mother is not in favor of my entering the seminary," and asking whether he could delay admission. Joseph wrote, "While she would not force her will upon me in such an important matter, nevertheless, she tries to dissuade me from entering. She will not succeed and she half knows it. I had hoped to enter the seminary this coming September. That would have given me plenty of time to make her see things my way, or to soften the blow a bit."[17] Despite those difficulties, however, Joseph entered St. Mary's College in Kentucky to begin his study for the priesthood in September 1945.

Compared to his classmates, Joseph began seminary at a disadvantage. Having spent his first year of college preparing to study medicine at the University of South Carolina and having attended a public high school, he had no Latin. At this time, twenty years before the Second Vatican Council, no one could be a priest without at least a working knowledge of that otherwise little-used language. In fact, even to study for the priesthood in those days demanded some Latin. It was for that reason that Walsh selected St. Mary's in Kentucky for the young seminarian, Joseph Bernardin. It was a place where Latin would be taught, rather than a place that assumed Latin was already known by seminarians. Joseph made rapid progress in his studies. His grade reports were uniformly excellent, and he was bold enough in April 1946 to write to Walsh that his Latin was better, asking whether he might study philosophy at The Catholic University of America in Washington, DC. Walsh sent him to St. Mary's in Baltimore instead, where he studied until 1948.

Still, Joseph would go to Washington. The diocesan chancellor, Msgr. John L. Manning, wrote to the rector of Theological College on the campus of Catholic University in February 1948 to plead for Joseph's admission. "This young man has made such good grades in his studies," wrote Manning, "that the Bishop would like to have him in Washington for theology, and at the same time to have him work for a Master's degree in Education at the Catholic University."[18] To pursue the degree in education was, in fact, Joseph's request. Walsh, through Manning, obliged happily, with Manning adding, "We have no doubt that he will be able to do this." Later, Joseph would find himself a teacher at Charleston's Bishop England High School and enmeshed in educational issues during his ministry as a bishop. His interest in education as a way of helping people was plain even at this early moment.

The academic work at Theological College was more challenging than the work Joseph had done at both St. Mary's. His grades reflect the greater challenge, especially in homiletics and even in scripture. Little surprise, though, that this man who would grow to become a consummate church administrator earned an A in Administrative Church Systems, shown on a January 1950 grade report. By March 1950 Joseph would apply to Charleston's new bishop, John Joyce Russell, for tonsure and admission to minor orders, and he was well on his way to the date of his ordination.

The arrival of Bishop Russell in Charleston was an important event in the priestly career of Joseph Bernardin, though no one could have known it in 1950. Edmund Walsh had been bishop of Charleston since before Joseph's birth, consecrated and installed in 1927 at the age of thirty-five. Walsh's assignment to Youngstown, Ohio, in 1950, the event that brought Russell to Charleston, ended more than two decades of stability in the Diocese of Charleston and precipitated a remarkable fifteen-year period that would see four bishops rotate in and out of the diocese by 1965. In his later years, upon his appointment to Atlanta as an auxiliary bishop, Joseph would look back to recall all that he had learned from the four bishops of Charleston he served as a priest. To have been made America's youngest Roman Catholic bishop, Joseph observed, was due to reasons "completely unrelated to personal qualities."[19] Rather, being a young priest of unusual administrative ability, Joseph had found himself in the right place at the right time—in a diocese that said goodbye to three bishops in seven years. Joseph Bernardin had been the indispensable man in the Diocese of Charleston, he had learned much from it, and church leaders had noticed.

But before any of that could begin, Joseph would need to be ordained a priest, which took place on April 26, 1952, at St. Joseph Catholic Church in Columbia. Preparations for that happy event began more than a year earlier, even before Joseph's ordination to the diaconate in October 1951 by Washington's Cardinal Patrick O'Boyle. In January 1951 St. Joseph's pastor Fr. Alfred Kamler began writing to Russell to secure an ordination date at St. Joseph. No doubt, the Bernardin family's Columbia roots had much to do with Kamler's insistence. Kamler renewed his request in November 1951. Still with no reply, perhaps in part to remind Russell, he wrote again on December 9, 1951, to ask whether Joseph might preach at Midnight Mass and distribute Communion while home from Theological College for Christmas. Thus, Joseph Bernardin preached his first homily at the Midnight Mass of 1951 (though Russell found "no grave reason for Mr. Bernardin to give Holy Communion").[20] Russell finally confirmed the ordination date in February 1952, and the ordination took place on Kamler's preferred date. Father Joseph Bernardin celebrated his first solemn High Mass the next day, the Third Sunday of Easter.

Joseph's first priestly assignment came at St. Joseph's in Columbia, where he had been ordained and where Kamler had been so keen to bring him on board. Columbia was comfortable for Joseph, near his mother and his sister, and by then St. Joseph was their home parish. Even these early years of his priesthood were not quiet. Before 1952 was over, Joseph was appointed the diocesan director of the CYO (Catholic Youth Organization) and the director of vocations. Even more unbelievably, in 1952 Joseph joined the faculty at Bishop England High School, located one hundred miles southeast of St. Joseph's, near Charleston. In those days when priests were more plentiful, Joseph's duties in Columbia at St. Joseph's probably were rather light. Perhaps he spent the week in Charleston at Bishop England and returned to Columbia for weekends. But what seems most clear is that Joseph, who had asked to study education while he was at Catholic University, was a priest whose ministry was being tailored to serve young people. That began to change after only a year, when Joseph was transferred in 1953 from St. Joseph's to the Cathedral of St. John the Baptist in Charleston. Perhaps the transfer was to ease Joseph's travel, but its effect was to bring him more closely into the administrative functions of the bishop's office, the chancery. Joseph kept his role as CYO director for another year, remained director of vocations until 1960, and became the chaplain to Catholic students at The Citadel, a military academy near Charleston, when he came to St. John the Baptist. While he was in Charleston, Russell began to notice that this young priest had a talent for administration. An abrupt change in the direction of his ministry would take place barely two years after Joseph's ordination, and that change of direction would be the first step in a pattern of increasing responsibility that followed him throughout the rest of his life. In 1954 Joseph would be appointed vice chancellor for the Diocese of Charleston, and he became chancellor in 1956. (In the language of the twenty-first century, a diocesan chancellor would be like a chief operating officer.) Just four years after his ordination, Joseph Bernardin was administrating the Diocese of Charleston on a day-to-day basis.

The event that would begin to shape the rest of Joseph's life took place on July 3, 1958, when word came that Russell would leave the Diocese of Charleston, having been appointed the bishop of Richmond in Virginia. As a result of Russell's leaving, Joseph would meet the man who became the eighth bishop of Charleston, Paul Hallinan. Hallinan became a mentor and a father figure to Joseph for the rest of his life and also would be responsible for his becoming a bishop. Hallinan was appointed bishop of Charleston on September 9, 1958, and first met Joseph about three weeks later in Richmond, at Russell's installation Mass. The two carried on an active correspondence between September and November, full of Hallinan's questions about the diocese and Joseph's detailed replies. Later, when Joseph looked back on this time, he was still "impressed with the new bishop's inquisitive mind and his desire to learn all he could" about the Diocese of Charleston.[21] Hallinan would be the second of four bishops to preside over Charleston between 1958 and 1964. All four would depend on Joseph's help, but Joseph would hold none in the affection he reserved for Hallinan.

Bishop Hallinan's curiosity about the diocese resonated well with young Joseph's detail-oriented work ethic. Joseph wrote appreciatively in 1962: "When Bishop Paul J. Hallinan first received notice of his appointment as the eighth Bishop of Charleston on September 9, 1958, South Carolina was little more than a name for him. . . . When he walked down the aisle of the Cathedral for his solemn Installation two months later, Hallinan had learned much more about the diocese."[22] Hallinan was a man accustomed to taking his work seriously. He began a PhD in history in 1953, many years before he came to Charleston. Progress on his degree was slowed considerably by his ministry as bishop, but Joseph recalled later how "Hallinan kept two desks in his study, one for diocesan business, the other for historical research to which, often late at night, he would turn his attention after he had fulfilled his episcopal responsibilities for the day."[23] Western Reserve University would award Hallinan's degree in 1963, ten years after he had begun it, making Hallinan the only sitting archbishop in history to earn a doctoral degree from an American university.

As time went on, it became clear that the affinity between Hallinan and Joseph would cover a lot more ground than just their serious devotion to hard work. Hallinan came to South Carolina as a northerner, born and raised in Ohio. His introduction to the American South of the midcentury included an indoctrination in its peculiar social structures. In his diary Hallinan recorded that visiting the parish in a small South Carolina city, he found "two Catholic churches, two schools, and two halls (one for whites and one for blacks), and he admitted that he found the reality of segregation even more confusing than the theory."[24] More disturbing, in 1959 Hallinan learned about Catholic hospitals turning away patients because they were African American. In a letter to the administrator of St. Francis Xavier hospital in Charleston, he described "a woman who was criticized in Confession because she did not have the fetus baptized in a miscarriage, and when asked by the priest why she had not gone to a Catholic hospital, had to reply: 'I couldn't— I'm Negro.'"[25] Confronted with these embarrassing injustices, Hallinan embarked on a firm course toward racial integration in his diocese. In Joseph he found a willing and helpful ally.

In an undated talk titled "The Church and the Negro," Joseph described the history of African American Catholics in South Carolina. Joseph pointed toward the work of nineteenth century bishops England and Lynch, as well as other efforts to reach out to African American Catholics. Joseph was rather frank about the prospects in his own time, at one point saying, "There will have to be a lot of soul-searching on the part of many white Catholics. Certainly the events of the past several years in the field of race relations have raised problems of conscience for many. Ultimately, in order to resolve these problems there will have to be a change of mind and heart. The virtues of justice and charity will not co-exist with some of the thinking that is now prevalent."[26]

A few years later, the Knights of Columbus posed a more pointed problem, and Joseph was perhaps even more pointed in reply. Resistance to integration of the Knights across the South had been so widespread that a separate organization was created for African American Catholics, the Knights of St. Peter Claver, which by 1950 had grown to 11,000 members.[27] Joseph delivered this message in person to the state council and local councils of the Knights for South Carolina:

> If we are going to stay in step with the Church; if we want to continue our status as an organization which is officially approved by the Church and one which works with the Church in accomplishing her mission, then we must face up to our moral responsibility in this matter and welcome as a member any Catholic men who qualifies [*sic*] according to the standards which have been accepted for membership in the past. While I am realistic enough to realize that such a policy will not immediately find acceptance by the entire membership, it is the only course of action which will bring honor to the Church and to the order.[28]

Certainly Joseph was encouraged by Hallinan's determination to integrate the Diocese of Charleston. But there can be little doubting Joseph's own instinctive inspiration to strike out against racial discrimination.

By 1960 Hallinan had resolved to pursue integration as speedily as prudent across the diocese. In a pastoral letter issued together with the bishops of Atlanta and Savannah, Hallinan promised that "Catholic pupils, regardless of color, will be admitted to Catholic schools as soon as this can be done with safety to the children and the school. Certainly this will be done not later than the public schools are opened to all pupils."[29] Joseph watched all of this unfold up close, observing the courage of Hallinan that marched hand in hand with pastoral sensitivity. Even as a time came when Joseph feared that Hallinan would waver under the pressure, Hallinan reassured him: "I have only started and I never give up."[30]

In 1961 Joseph became the director of Catholic cemeteries for the Diocese of Charleston. Being a leader in the church is not only a matter of writing homilies and pastoral letters, after all. The church has more practical needs that come with attending to the spiritual needs of people or confronting social injustices. Schools and hospitals, shelters and soup kitchens do not just support themselves. They require stewardship. Joseph had a chance to learn this sort of stewardship when he was faced daily with the responsibilities of making business decisions as the director of cemeteries.

Before 1962 ended, two important things happened. Hallinan left Charleston, having been appointed archbishop of Atlanta. But before Hallinan left Charleston, it seems that he had arranged for Joseph to be named Domestic Prelate of His Holiness—in plainer English, barely ten years after his ordination, Joseph now was Msgr. Bernardin at the tender age of thirty-four. The title probably was a sign of Hallinan's personal regard for Joseph as much as it was the traditional reward in those days for a priest who had built a new parish building or, in this case, one who had opened a new cemetery. The year 1962 would be another one of uncertainty in Charleston as Hallinan gave way to Bishop Francis Reh, and the transition would bring another opportunity for Joseph to demonstrate his administrative skill.

Bishop Reh was named to the Diocese of Charleston on June 4, 1962, and installed on July 18. Scarcely two months later, Reh named Joseph as vicar general for the diocese. In canon law, the vicar general is second in authority only to the bishop. (Thinking of the diocesan chancellor as a chief operating officer, the vicar general like a chief executive officer.) In Catholic theology, a bishop holds three offices as the shepherd of his diocese—to teach, to sanctify, and to govern. The vicar general is the bishop's primary assistant with respect to governing and, for Joseph Bernardin, this opportunity to govern in Reh's name came at an important time. The Second Vatican Council kept Reh out of Charleston for long stretches. Reh's lengthy absences left his young vicar general in charge of the Diocese of Charleston. For the period while he was in Rome at the council, Reh delegated to Joseph the authority:

- to appoint parochial vicars & assistants
- to remove parochial vicars
- to issue dismissorial letters
- to inflict penalties *ad homine*
- to absolve in external forum apostates, heretics, and schismatics.[31]

Needless to say, Joseph's authority covered a lot of ground! Certainly, the list demonstrated that Joseph was growing accustomed to governing a diocese much as a bishop does—and his fortieth birthday was most of a decade away. As his father's death left Joseph with a lot of responsibility for his family at a young age, here again Joseph exercised responsibility for the pastoral needs of a diocese at an age when many priests still were living in their first rectory.

Circumstances beyond his control put Joseph in that position of responsibility. The quick succession of bishops, from Russell to Hallinan to Reh, was one thing. But the Second Vatican Council opened wide the doors and windows to the world for Joseph Bernardin as much as it did for the church. The council met in Rome for four sessions from 1962–1965, each session lasting about two or three months. In practical terms, accounting for travel time and time spent in Rome preparing for sessions to begin, this meant that Reh was away from his Charleston diocese for five of the twenty-six months he was bishop. While it was true that during this period Reh took the unusual step of appointing Msgr. Martin Murphy to be co-vicar general ("when the territory of a diocese is extensive, Canon Law allows the appointment of more than one Vicar General"), Joseph found himself spending much of the conciliar period functioning as a bishop.[32] Perhaps it was with this in mind that Joseph would recall later that his "entire episcopal ministry has taken place in [the Council's] shadow."[33] Indeed, in a way we can say it began with the council.

That observation raises another point. Joseph was ordained in 1952, and he was a priest for ten years before the council even began. Perhaps it is difficult to imagine Joseph Bernardin chanting in Latin at the Mass while facing away from the people, but it happened many times during his young priesthood. He was a well-established priest when the council began. Those who knew him as a young priest remember his presidential style at Mass was formal, even a bit rote, in the style of the pre-Vatican II liturgy. Already, he was a monsignor when the council began, and many men in the priesthood would be comfortably set in their ways by that time. Yet Joseph embraced the council. The event transformed his ministry and his life. That transformation could be seen in the change that came over his celebration of the Mass, after he had grown through the council into "an effective preacher and presider."[34] Joseph's close relationship with Hallinan helps this make more sense. Hallinan was a passionate advocate for liturgical reform, and his years as bishop of Charleston were "a period during which an intensive effort was made to give the laity a greater appreciation of the significance and beauty of the liturgy," beginning in 1958 even before Pope John called for an ecumenical council.[35] Hallinan understood keenly that "the chief transformation" that would accompany the liturgical renewal would be one having an effect on the people "*personally*, on the *parish*, on the *Church*."[36] Joseph was moved by the liturgical renewal, and by the way it transformed life inside the church. Shortly after the council, he said, "Within the framework which has been established by lawful authority, we should always be looking for new, imaginative ways of making the Liturgy more understandable, more relevant to our lives."[37]

It was more than renewal of the liturgy or changes in the church that animated Joseph during these critical years. Opportunities for contact between the Roman Catholic Church and other religious traditions, brought out of the shadows by the council, seized Joseph's imagination and would stay with him for the rest of his life. "My vision," he said, "certainly has been expanded as a result of Vatican II."[38] He embraced a spirit of reconciliation at a meeting of the Council of Churches in Beaufort, South Carolina, around 1965, describing a "new spirit of fraternal charity" that made it possible for the church "to admit that, because of the frail human element in the Church, we are as responsible as anyone else for the difficulties which have resulted in a divided Christendom."[39] Over time he extended that reconciling impulse not only to include fellow Christians, but to launch an extraordinary outreach to the Jewish community that culminated in his historic journey to Israel in 1995. All of this began in Joseph's willing "yes" to the council, his assent of mind and spirit that changed his priesthood and charted a course for the rest of his life.

In 1965 barely two years after arriving in Charleston, Reh left to become rector of the Pontifical North American College in Rome. A new bishop arrived, the last bishop Joseph would know as a Charleston priest and the bishop who would bring Joseph to be a part of the final session of the Second Vatican Council. For this transition, Joseph was named the administrator for the Diocese of Charleston.

Bishop Unterkoefler would remain in Charleston until his retirement in 1990 and, though he reappointed Joseph to be vicar general, Joseph would not be in Charleston for much longer. In late 1965 Joseph was away from the diocese to attend the final session of the Second Vatican Council as an assistant to Unterkoefler. Only a few short months later, he would depart for Atlanta. Joseph wrote about the Second Vatican Council in the decades that would follow, but very little about his own experience apart from pointing out that "I never spoke during the sessions and I had no role in the work. . . . I was overwhelmed, and I wondered why I had been invited, but I was delighted to be there."[40]

Archbishop Paul Hallinan of Atlanta, Joseph's friend and mentor who had been bishop of Charleston, contracted a severe liver infection during the first session of the council. His illness had left him unable to administrate the archdiocese on his own, and his petition for an auxiliary bishop was granted. Joseph would leave Charleston in 1966 to become auxiliary bishop and rector of the Atlanta Cathedral. A new era was beginning in the church, and a new era for Joseph Bernardin, too. Having spent fourteen years gradually taking on more and more responsibility, he was ready to become the youngest Catholic bishop in the United States.

He would tell the story many more times throughout his life about the day when he was ordained a bishop. "My mother and I happened to meet each other outside the Charleston Cathedral about an hour before the episcopal consecration began," he would remember. "After making a few remarks about the festivities that were soon to follow, she gave me this advice: 'Now, Joe, when the ceremony begins, walk straight and don't look too pleased.'"[41] Joseph certainly was ready to become a bishop, whether or not he was pleased.

Maria Simion Bernardin, an Italian immigrant widowed with two children only six years after she arrived in the United States, surely beamed at the man her son, Joe, had become.

CHAPTER TWO

The Youngest Bishop in America
(1966–72)

At the time when Paul J. Hallinan was installed as the bishop of Charleston in 1958, Joseph had been one of the priests living at the bishop's house. Years later he told the story of talking with a longtime housekeeper at the house and saying to her, "It looks as if we are getting a good man [Hallinan]. I'm sure we will like him." The housekeeper replied, "We've got to like him, because he's the only one we are going to get." It is safe to say that the people of Charleston not only liked Hallinan, but they grew to love him. Perhaps none grew to love him more than Joseph Bernardin.

To compare the lives of Paul Hallinan and Joseph Bernardin side by side can suggest something about how and why these two men grew to be like father and son. Hallinan was born seventeen years earlier than Bernardin, almost to the day, in Painesville, Ohio. Though Ohio was a northern state and Painesville only thirty miles from Cleveland, life in Painesville was sleepy to the point of being rural. Painesville could boast a longstanding Catholic community, even if it was a small one, much like Columbia, South Carolina. Anti-Catholic bigotry was not unknown in Painesville, though Hallinan enjoyed a contented childhood at the center of a large, loving family. Hallinan's story departs considerably from Bernardin's in early adulthood. At a time in life when Joseph was discerning whether to become a priest and beginning to study medicine at the University of South Carolina, Hallinan had determined to join the priesthood and studied at Notre Dame. But Hallinan's experiences as a chaplain in the Pacific theater during World War II gave him a perspective on life and suffering probably not much different from the one Bernardin had gotten through hard lessons of his own. In fact, both men had begun their priesthood with ministries to youth—Bernardin as a high school teacher and CYO chaplain, Hallinan with CYO work in his first parish and later as a Newman Club chaplain in Cleveland and national chaplain for Newman organizations. Finally, both men came somewhat improbably to the senior levels of church leadership—Joseph, despite not having studied in Rome, and Hallinan who, as Joseph recalled, was "surprised that he had been made a bishop, genuinely surprised, unlike some clerics who affect shock and dismay when they receive the mitre that they had confidently expected."[1]

When Archbishop Hallinan died in 1968, segregationist Gov. Lester Maddox and Rev. Martin Luther King, Jr. sat together in the front pew for the funeral Mass at Atlanta's Cathedral of Christ the King. King would be assassinated only days later, and the rancor between the two men was such that Maddox did not attend King's funeral and refused to close state offices to mourn the occasion. They had overcome all that to sit next to each other to honor Hallinan, and Joseph recalled later, "Only a man like Hallinan could have brought those two together."[2] Hallinan was the sort of man who could win admiration from just about everyone. A contemporary, Bishop James Shannon of the Archdiocese of Saint Paul-Minneapolis, memorialized him this way: "Persons who were privileged to be his friends will never forget the impact of his personality. It was his mission in life to encourage others who lacked his buoyancy and *joi de vivre*. He was a naturally happy man, and a smile his most characteristic feature."[3] Even more than this joyful spirit, people admired Hallinan's courage and determination. Joseph would remember him, in his funeral Mass homily, for his humanness and his courage. Paul Hallinan arrived in the South in 1958 already aware he would need to address the injustice of racial discrimination. He never wavered from that path. In another context the distinguished historian of American Catholicism (and good friend of Hallinan's) John Tracy Ellis recalled Hallinan's spirited campaign for liturgical renewal during the Second Vatican Council. "On one of my visits to him in Atlanta," Ellis recalled, Hallinan "showed me—with the merry twinkle so characteristic of this fun-loving man's eyes—a colored shapshot of Cardinal Spellman and himself. . . . The archbishop's arm was thrust forward in an emphatic gesture before the cardinal whose grave countenance reflected a mixture of puzzlement and annoyance." Spellman was known to be an opponent of liturgical reform, even as Hallinan was a leader among Americans seeking a reformed liturgy. Ellis concluded: "It would not have occurred to Paul Hallinan that by arguing with the powerful cardinal in the presence of their episcopal colleagues he was taking his ecclesiastical life in his hands."[4] Paul Hallinan, happy warrior, championed the causes that were dear to him cautiously, but with little care for the cost to himself and, in this way, it is notable that Joseph remembered Hallinan as "my teacher, my counsellor, my friend."[5]

It was at the first and second sessions of the Second Vatican Council where the council fathers debated and approved *Sacrosanctum Concilium* (Constitution on the Sacred Liturgy), which Pope Paul VI promulgated on December 4, 1963. In those sessions, which met in Rome during the autumns of 1962 and 1963, Hallinan emerged as a leader among the Americans and became friends with Detroit's Archbishop John Dearden. But Hallinan's return from the council in December of 1963 proved to be a tragic turning point in his life—and in Joseph's.

While vacationing in Ohio for the Christmas holiday, Hallinan became severely ill. He returned promptly to Atlanta, and his physician admitted him to St. Joseph's Infirmary where the archbishop of Atlanta spent the next 270 days suffering from what eventually would prove to be a fatal hepatitis infection probably contracted during his time in Rome. Hallinan would recover his strength during periods of time over the next five years. He missed the third session of the council, though he managed to attend the fourth and final session. He remained an active correspondent with Dearden as well as with Philadelphia's Archbishop John Krol about the council. He was pleased to be one of only two Americans appointed to the Vatican's *Consilium* that would plan for the implementation of liturgical renewal, even if he was generally unable to meet with the group. As 1964 headed toward 1965, Hallinan was permitted only four hours of work per day by his physicians, and he would not resume a regular workday for the rest of his life. It was clear to him that he was going to need help.

Throughout Hallinan's early years in Atlanta, which were also the earliest years of his illness, he and Joseph remained in touch. Joseph had visited Hallinan "a number of times during his long illness," and we know that Hallinan retained a high opinion of his diocesan chancellor from Charleston. Seemingly unbeknownst to Joseph, by early 1966 Hallinan had gone so far as to request that the Holy See grant him an auxiliary bishop, and he had told the apostolic delegate, Archbishop Vagnozzi, that he hoped it would be Joseph. The Archdiocese of Atlanta was not nearly so large in those days as it has become in the early twenty-first century, and an auxiliary bishop in such a small archdiocese was extraordinary. However, the apostolic delegate had a good relationship with Hallinan and recognized the severity of the situation. Vagnozzi gave assurances that Hallinan would be able to pick his own man. Hallinan did, and Rome approved.

The only person who seemed to be in the dark about it was Joseph Bernardin. In March 1966 Joseph had been preparing to leave Charleston for one of his visits with Hallinan, when:

> several hours before I left my office in Charleston to board the plane, the letter arrived from the Apostolic Delegate in Washington informing me that Pope Paul VI intended to name me auxiliary to Archbishop Hallinan. I was told that I should wire back my acceptance. . . . After sending the requested telegram of acceptance, I boarded the plane and was met at the Atlanta airport by the Archbishop who knew, of course, that an auxiliary was to be appointed but did not know that I had already been notified. Needless to say, he was very pleased when I gave him the news.[6]

That event drew Joseph out of the local church in Charleston for the first time and into a much bigger world. Joseph was ready to greet that world.

At his Mass of reception in Atlanta on May 4, 1966, Bishop Bernardin offered an expansive address full of big ideas. "The times in which we live are not ordinary times," he said.[7] He went on to talk about the remarkable changes taking place and, while he did not name them all, offering the list hardly was necessary. Leaving aside the changes taking place in the church, there were the remarkable technological, social, and political changes taking place everywhere around the world. Joseph had read the signs of the times closely and saw "a new spirit" at work, one "which has jolted our complacency."[8] But Joseph did focus his attention on the church, gave tribute to Pope John and the Second Vatican Council, and then offered this remarkable ecclesial vision:

> The Church, while ever remaining a society with the structures and laws common to all societies, is fundamentally the presence of God's merciful action among men. The Church, in other words, is *people*. . . . Everything, therefore, which deserves the name Christian must be geared toward helping—toward serving—God's people. . . . It is within this context that the role of a Bishop must be understood. Moreover, his mission is to all men, not just to those who are registered as Catholics and people will respond to him if they see in his life and in his service to others the image of Christ, the Good Shepherd.[9]

In the words of the episcopal motto he just had chosen, "As Those Who Serve," Joseph came to Atlanta as a bishop who was cognizant and confident of being a bishop in an age of renewal. He had fully absorbed the spirit and the meaning of the council. Joseph had, in the dawning months after its closing, become a bishop of the council.

How is it that Joseph made the difficult transition from his preconciliar priesthood to his postconciliar episcopacy? Many priests did not have such an easy time. Those who did often were scholars, steeped in the debates over liturgical renewal or ecumenism, or they were priests who had spent their lives in pastoral work, close to the people of God and alert to their most urgent concerns about the faith. Joseph had his academic training, but he never was a scholar. He barely was ever a parish priest. Where in Joseph did this openness to renewal and reform find its beginning? How did this devoted churchman whose priesthood had been preoccupied by transacting the church's business and enforcing the church's rules come to be the servant-leader who set himself in the midst of God's people and put their needs before everything else?

The only answer can be that it was something in Joseph Bernardin—whether he had become a bishop or not, whether he had become a priest or not. Joseph's character and personality, the depths of his soul, were revealed by his response to the Second Vatican Council and the beginning of his episcopal ministry. In the same way that Libby Bernardin recalled the gentleness of the Bernardin men or in a way much like the people of Tonadico di Primiero had cultivated openness to one another's cultural differences across centuries, Joseph met the new spirit of the age in which he lived with arms wide open, with a ready smile, and with a firm commitment to bringing forth the reign of God.

Together in Atlanta, Joseph and Hallinan worked together to forge a visionary program not only for implementation of the council, but for a renewed place for the church in dialogue with the modern world. Hallinan had such plans well underway by the time Joseph received his episcopal consecration in April, 1966. With the council now concluded, Hallinan had turned his attention toward thinking about the governance of his archdiocese in a new light. Specifically, Hallinan was eager to call an archdiocesan synod, a mechanism provided under canon law to bring together the clergy of a diocese or archdiocese to be heard by and to consult with the local ordinary. Hallinan wanted such a gathering, but with the promises of Vatican II ringing so fresh in every ear, he sought to avoid having a meeting only for priests. To evade the requirement of canon law that a synod was only for priests, he determined to call a laypersons' congress ahead of the synod. Hallinan sought "to provide a true channel for lay opinion, initiative, and participation," and invited thirty laypeople to make recommendations for the synod.[10] Those appointees gave way eventually to elected representatives from parishes who then convened on May 20. The response from the laity of Atlanta was so overwhelming that additional congresses were convened. Before the actual synod opened in November, a sisters' congress for women religious and a young adults' congress also took place.[11] Though only priests could participate in the synod, Hallinan invited every Catholic in the archdiocese to attend so that "the decree that [the synod] will produce will be *of* God's people, *by* God's people and *for* God's people."[12] And though Hallinan cut off a discussion of priestly celibacy, he could take credit for creating an open environment in which a priests' senate, sisters' council, and elected parish councils came to be part of the archdiocesan model of governance. Joseph arrived in Atlanta while all this was already underway, but the preparations for and execution of this synod give some idea of the environment in which he found himself as a new auxiliary bishop.

Not only an auxiliary bishop, Joseph also was vicar general and rector of the Cathedral of Christ the King. "At Christ the King," he would say, "Even before 'team ministries' became popular, we worked together as a team."[13] We can imagine that the new environment for the church in Atlanta cultivated by Hallinan, with its emphasis on participation, was a happy one for Joseph. It also is worth observing that his two years at Christ the King were his first years of parish ministry since St. Joseph in Columbia, when he was first ordained. They also would be, practically, his last years in parish ministry. He would recall later that this was the hardest part about leaving Atlanta in 1968 because, "I liked parish work more than diocesan administration," and for that reason, he resisted his appointment to the National Conference of Catholic Bishops "for as long as I could because I preferred to stay in diocesan ministry."[14] Joseph must have enjoyed his work at Christ the King parish very much, since the record of his life attests to his considerable aptitude for administration, even looking all the way back to his seminary grades.

Surely at least some of that enjoyment is from the times in which Joseph had an opportunity to be a pastor. These were the earliest years of implementation and experimentation with liturgical renewal, of which Hallinan was a national, arguably global, leader. Renewal did not come all at once. The reform had been underway as early as the 1940s, and plans were being crafted in Rome for further changes at the time when the council was convened by Pope John XXIII. The energy of the changes began to gather and focus the attention of Catholics in the mid-1960s when some portions of the Mass began to be heard in local languages or when the eucharistic prayers began to be recited facing the people. But as quickly as liturgical change came, divisions of opinion over the changes emerged and multiplied to a degree that still is with the church today. As the rector of the Atlanta cathedral, Joseph had charge over the cathedral parish and was responsible to implement the changes as much as to deal with people's sensitivities about the Mass. Joseph cultivated high hopes for the ability of a participatory liturgy to affect "minds, hearts, and wills so that when we come together to celebrate the Eucharist we are conscious of the bond of love which unites us," and for a liturgy that would escape "the very real danger of identifying the liturgy, which is our worship of God, with the rubrics, which are the rules or guides which are intended to help us conduct our worship in a meaningful way."[15] Joseph was clear eyed about the difficulty. Just a few years after the council he expressed a worry that the liturgical renewal was not succeeding to unify Catholics, still not freeing worshippers from a formalism that substituted an idea for worship for worship itself. But his active concern stayed with the problem.

Probably Joseph had in mind his own experiences at the Cathedral of Christ the King a few years later when he wrote that theologians of liturgy run a double risk. Either they will be "dangerous innovators or dangerous conservators" in the search for a delicate balance between continuity and discontinuity, respecting the people's comfort with the old liturgical style while still addressing the church to the modern world and making necessary updates.[16] This was the substance of what Joseph had spoken about in his Mass of reception when he came to Atlanta in 1966, the "new spirit" that has "jolted our complacency." Change, the necessity of change, and the hazards of change were in the air of the 1960s and certainly dominated Joseph's time in parish ministry while in Atlanta. Those changes, as Joseph observed when he came to Atlanta in 1966, were as much at work in the church as anywhere else in the world. Frequently, though, the church and the world came into contact over those changes.

For example, only five months after arriving in Atlanta, Joseph and Hallinan jointly released a pastoral letter that confronted the Vietnam conflict directly, at a time when Gallup polling found that barely half (54 percent) of the

American people thought the United States had made a mistake introducing troops to combat in that far-off country. There had been some pressure for the US Catholic bishops to say something about the war. The *New York Times* noted, critically, that the bishops had "largely been silent or, in the case of several leaders such as Cardinal Spellman of New York, supported the war effort," but that, "The position of the American Catholic hierarchy . . . contrasts sharply with the peace efforts of Pope Paul."[17] Perhaps in reply to sentiments like those, Baltimore's Cardinal Shehan issued his own pastoral letter in the summer that cautiously urged the US government to observe the requirements of just war theory. But Hallinan and Joseph went somewhat further in their October, 1966 letter, "War and Peace."

In terms that recall the new spirit of the 1960s and the challenges that accompanied it, "War and Peace" challenges conventional ideas and invites the reader to think in a new way suited to a new time. Hallinan and Bernardin observed the difference between "true patriotism," which "does not end at a nation's borders, and "false patriotism," characterized by "a narrowing of mind . . . racial prejudice and bitter nationalism." They urged Christians to raise their voices "against the savagery and terror of war." They called on the US government to pursue "vigorously, wholeheartedly, and repeatedly every opening which has even the slightest hope of peaceful settlement."[18] Alongside questions of war and peace came questions of protest and civil disobedience. In a 1968 interview with the *Denver Register*, Joseph spoke of his support for a conscientious right to peaceful civil disobedience. But a more interesting challenge arose in August 1966 when two Atlanta priests participated in a Hiroshima Day walk commemorating the American atomic bombing of Japan in connection with a protest against the war in Vietnam. Joseph's statement to the press was characteristically measured, noting first that the priests had made their protests "as individuals, not as official spokesmen for the Archdiocese," but going on to note that "it is legitimate—even necessary—to discuss the fact and the degree of the involvement of the United States in this war so that we will never lose our moral perspective."[19] Throughout his episcopal ministry, Joseph made several statements like these, finding a careful middle ground where the legitimate voices of all parties could be heard. We can see the influence of his mentor, Hallinan, who wrote that to be a bishop in the midcentury demanded, "Balance and restraint, study and testing, dialogue and the mature shouldering of responsibility."[20] But Joseph himself may have summed it up best when a reporter tried to pin him down, asking whether he was a liberal, a conservative, a liberal-conservative, a conservative-liberal, and so forth, and Joseph replied simply, "I shun labels. I think they can be very misleading."[21] Truth, Joseph believed, is found in being more discerning.

No greater challenge to Joseph's instincts toward conciliation and justice arose during those years than the struggle for civil rights. As a native southerner, Joseph knew the problem well and had seen up close the efforts of Hallinan, Reh, and Unterkoefler to respond to it. But those years in Atlanta, 1966–1968, brought some of the most difficult moments in the history of the civil rights movement. Because Atlanta was home to Dr. King, that city was a focus of national attention. On this issue, there was less room for nuance or restraint than the questions of war and peace. When Hallinan gave permission for six priests to march in Selma in 1965, he gave this remarkable statement: "There are times when we must risk safety and convenience and protocol—and even lives. This was one of those times—and six priests from our archdiocese took part in the protest. We thank God that they are home safe, and we thank Him too that they took part. Someone recently called me 'that Nigger-loving Archbishop.' If I were not, I would be untrue to the motto 'That you may love one another' [his episcopal motto]. When we all follow this command of Christ, there will be no further need for demonstrations."[22]

Just as it was in Charleston when Joseph called on the Knights of Columbus to accept African American members, his role was to stand next to the archbishop and push force-fully for change during this period. Though the Atlanta Catholic schools already had been integrated by the time Joseph got there, integration still was controversial enough at the time of his appointment that it was among only a few issues discussed in his first interview with the archdiocesan newspaper. Perhaps especially because of Hallinan's illness, Joseph's work as vicar general for the archdiocese involved him in some of the more sensitive issues of integration. Southern bishops for decades had accommodated the South's system of segregation by setting some parishes aside sepa-rately for African Americans. During a phase of parish merg-ers and re-organization in 1967, Joseph proposed that a new, experimental parish community be merged with an estab-lished African American parish. This problem had come up in the desegregation of Charleston parishes, too: while es-tablished, African American parishes were a shameful re-minder of segregation, they also were thriving communities where families had made a home for generations. Paradox-ically, and this was one of the more subtle and difficult prob-lems of the decade, the loss of those communities sometimes was more than families could bear, even in the name of a great good like integration. Joseph withdrew his proposal, and the African American parish remained.[23]

Joseph's proposal to merge that African American parish may not be a good example of Joseph's instincts toward conciliation, but withdrawing the proposal without any fuss was. Peaceableness and peace seeking were signature characteristics of Joseph's ministry, and they came to be more visibly a part of his work first during these years in Atlanta. Joseph's commitment to peace could be seen in his pastoral letter on the Vietnam War. But peaceableness was a thread woven into Joseph's life, even down to the level of humbly withdrawing a proposal to merge parishes because it threatened to spur conflict. The people of Atlanta noticed. When Joseph left Atlanta after two short years, the Catholic community recalled that "a spirit and a motive which ran through the statements of Bishop Bernardin while he was here among us was his concern for peace in our world."[24]

These two influential years of Joseph's ministry also brought another signature concern front and center. In Atlanta Joseph became active with interfaith and ecumenical work to a degree that had not been possible while he was a priest in Charleston. Very much in the spirit of the council's declarations, Joseph committed the Archdiocese of Atlanta to doing "everything in our power, both on the local and national level, to resist every form of anti-Semitism, no matter where it is found, whether inside the Church or outside."[25] Just like his commitment to peacefulness, Joseph's growing interfaith commitment was evidence of a personality that sought conciliation. But it also was evidence of Paul Hallinan's influence on him who, in a 1965 pastoral letter, had written that, "Our bond with the Jews is of a special historic nature," and that, "We are in some way a continuation of the chosen people of Israel, not only because Jesus and his apostles were Jews but because the covenant of the Old Testament was the first Catholic charter."[26]

Yet, it should be remembered that Hallinan's and Bernardin's partnership was a two-way street. Bernardin's role in the Archdiocese of Atlanta was well defined. The archbishop was ill; Joseph was to be the vicar general and to act for the archbishop where necessary. Hallinan's biographer records how Hallinan's "heart was clearly not in" administrative work, and how in Charleston "he was happy to leave day-to-day administration largely in the capable hands of Bernardin."[27] When Bernardin came to Atlanta, largely he resumed the role in Hallinan's life "that he had played in Charleston."[28] On the other hand, having become a bishop and attending the meetings of the National Conference of Catholic Bishops (NCCB) in Washington, Joseph was building his own national profile, meeting important Catholic leaders outside the Archdiocese of Atlanta and well beyond the South. When Joseph spoke about resisting anti-Semitism on the national level, he spoke credibly as a growing national leader of the Catholic church in the United States only as a result of having come to Atlanta.

Joseph's talents had attracted the attention of Hallinan's good friend, Detroit Archbishop John Dearden, who began a term as president of the NCCB in 1966. Sensing a capable administrator in Joseph who could be useful to his work at the NCCB in Washington, DC, Dearden began lobbying Hallinan to release Joseph for work at the NCCB. Hallinan's illness waxed and waned during these years, and in November 1967 Hallinan was feeling so robust that he agreed to let Joseph go. But a severe setback a few months later forced Hallinan to retract his promise in a frank and touching letter to Dearden:

> Now the entire situation has changed almost totally. I grew progressively worse after Christmas. . . . The sum-total of the matter is that, although after six months I'll be able

to carry on a little work, right now I simply *can't*. Obviously, I am trying to keep this quiet, but only Joe's fine, quiet work (with priests, finances and administrative matters) has made this possible. What this adds up to, John, is that I must withdraw my earlier promise, given to you in good faith. Dr. Wilber and I agree that to lose Bishop Bernardin would be the next step to the end for me.[29]

The proof of Bernardin's growing national stature and his devotion to assisting Hallinan can be found in the archives of the Archdiocese of Atlanta, where a stack of invitations to events outside Atlanta can be found with copies of Joseph's polite declines. From late 1967 until Hallinan's death in March 1968, Joseph appears to have devoted all of his energies to allaying any fears Hallinan may have had for his archdiocese by making sure it was managed well.

Joseph spurned Dearden's offers twice. Joseph recalled later that it was because he was so reluctant to leave pastoral work behind, his parish ministry in the cathedral, though there are good reasons to believe that his reluctance had at least as much to do with loyalty to Hallinan and a desire to minister to him in his final days. In his homily for the late archbishop, Joseph recalled a note Hallinan had written to him from the hospital shortly after learning that he would die: "Our last two conversations have brought me a serenity that I have lacked. Since you know me so well, this does not require another statement—that I am as determined and probably as stubborn as ever; with the same lack of fear of consequences when I am sure; the same will to live coupled (I hope) with a Christian acceptance of death, I'm not sure whether this acceptance includes suffering, pain, remorse, rejection, or disorientation."[30] Leaving everything else aside, and when all is said and done, Joseph was a priest, and Hallinan was a dying man. It is clear that Joseph had a ministry to this dying man, one who was so important not only for the advancement of his priestly career but whose personality and ecclesial vision shaped so much of who Joseph would become. Joseph ministered to Hallinan, brought serenity to a dying father. The experience, to all appearances, was important for both of them.

Once Hallinan had died, and the funeral rites had been completed, events moved quickly for Joseph. He became administrator of the Archdiocese while Atlanta awaited word of the appointment of a new archbishop from Rome. In the days just before Hallinan died, and as it was clear time was short, Joseph agreed to go to the NCCB in Washington once his work in Atlanta was completed. But only three days after Hallinan's funeral and before any public announcement of Joseph's eventual move to Washington could be made, Martin Luther King, Jr. was killed in Memphis. King, who sat in the front pew at Hallinan's funeral Mass, was a native of Atlanta and the events thrust Joseph into a position of national leadership. Joseph paid a call on Coretta Scott King, an event that he recalled with intensity after many years. A substantial profile of Joseph went out from the press department of the United States Catholic Conference shortly after word of his appointment to Washington was announced. Joseph's interviewer noticed his deep sunburn and asked whether Joseph was an avid golfer. Very gently, Joseph told him: "It came from marching in the funeral of Dr. Martin Luther King, Jr. Archbishop (John F.) Dearden (of Detroit and president of the USCC and NCCB) and I marched together in Dr. King's funeral procession."[31]

Dearden and Joseph marched together in that procession as national representatives of the Roman Catholic Church, the president of the bishops' conference, and the incoming general secretary. And, perhaps as might be expected after the loss of Hallinan, with John Dearden Joseph found another partner and mentor who would continue to shape his life and ministry.

Joseph's new position in Washington was, in a way, two positions. Particularly at the moment when Joseph came to Washington, the bishops' conference had a sort of tangled history. A meeting of a nation's Catholic bishops is a fairly new concept. American bishops met together a handful of times during the nineteenth century under the name of plenary councils. During World War I, those meetings were formalized somewhat and called the National Catholic War Council, where bishops met to collaborate toward aiding the war effort. Once the war ended, the bishops continued this arrangement and in 1919 created an organization called the National Catholic Welfare Council. The bishops met once annually as the NCWC, and slowly a bureaucratic organization grew up around it in Washington to aid the bishops' work. The Second Vatican Council clarified the work of bishops' conferences and provided specific tasks and duties for those organizations. In 1966 the NCWC became the National Conference of Catholic Bishops (NCCB). The NCCB was an organization in which the bishops could collaborate over matters internal to the church, such as the translation of the liturgy into English. At the same time in 1966, the bishops created the United States Catholic Conference (USCC), a separate, parallel organization through which the bishops would speak to the world outside the church on social issues like labor and on political issues like war and peace. Joseph would be the general secretary of the NCCB/USCC, the person in charge of both organizations' daily operations. Cardinal Dearden was the president of the NCCB/USCC and was ultimately responsible to the nation's bishops for what happened at the

NCCB/USCC. Joseph and Dearden worked closely together, formed a lasting relationship, over bringing the NCCB/USCC up to date in the light of the council's requirements.

From April until June of 1968, Joseph split his time between Atlanta and Washington, commuting by airplane. Joseph wrote about spending "the first half of the week in Washington and the second half in Atlanta," which he described as "an almost impossible situation."[32] With the assistance of the chancery staff he had worked with since 1966 in Atlanta, Joseph managed his duties to the archdiocese until Archbishop Thomas Donnellan arrived and was installed to succeed Hallinan. Meanwhile, there was a lot for Joseph to become familiar with in Washington at the NCCB/USCC.

The bishops' conference had been operating under rules adopted in 1922, even as the organization had grown increasingly complex. By the time Joseph arrived in 1968, the conference had developed a number of offices and accumulated a small but somewhat disorganized staff. More important, the Second Vatican Council had recognized the existence of bishops' conferences and identified a procedure by which they could make "juridically binding" decisions—that is to say, decisions that can be enforced under canon law. The conference had outgrown the 1922 statutes, but the American bishops were not really convinced that new statutes were needed. In Rome, the Vatican office with authority over bishops' conferences, the Sacred Congregation for Bishops, had different ideas. The problem came up promptly after Joseph's arrival in Washington in a memorandum written to his attention, which observed: "Since the first meeting of the NCCB in 1966, no further work has been done" to write new statutes for the Conference.[33] Joseph's handwritten notes at the bottom of the page indicate his desire to move forward, noting that "articles are appearing" in newspapers, and the bishops "should be ahead of the game," since Rome wanted to see a revised structure for the conference. Joseph made a note: "Write to [Cardinal John] Krol," who at that time was vice president of the conference. Joseph intended to move forward on the question of bringing the NCCB/USCC forward into a new era.

The question of modernizing the conference was more complex than it might at first seem. Nearly every American bishop had attended the Second Vatican Council, which had emphasized the principle of collegiality among bishops. Collegiality describes the concept of bishops working together collaboratively, less like individual medieval princes than like disciples of Jesus gathered around the same table. Joseph was committed to the principle of collegiality, a commitment he had shared with Hallinan and also with Dearden. In principle, every bishop agreed about collegiality and about bishops' conferences being the natural way for bishops to collaborate, just as the council had urged them to do. But changing bishops' habits and making it all happen was something quite different. An exchange of letters between Joseph and Dearden a few months into Joseph's time as general secretary illustrates this well. Joseph wrote to Dearden with some apparent frustration:

> I am writing in reference to the revision of the Statutes of our Conference. You will recall that on several occasions we have discussed the matter. Last month in Rome, for example, you suggested that perhaps it would be wise to appoint a committee which could work with Cardinal Krol who now has responsibility for working on the Statutes. . . . I should like to make a suggestion. I am somewhat reluctant to establish another committee. . . . Would it not be better for our staff to bring together what already exists

and to incorporate into that any new items which are needed? . . . The only problem with this is that someone will have to speak to Cardinal Krol and suggest that we follow this procedure. I spoke to the Cardinal in February and at that time offered my assistance. He appreciated the offer but indicated that before he would ask me to assist, there was some work he wanted to do personally. I have not heard from him since then.[34]

Work on the new statutes that would permit a greater spirit of collaboration had stalled because one cardinal had taken the matter into his own hands. Diplomatically, Joseph reminded Dearden that he, a new bishop, was unable to raise the matter again with Krol, a cardinal. Dearden, who grew to share Joseph's desire to press on the statutes, intervened with Krol, and the project moved forward quickly.

Joseph recalled about Dearden that "I must admit that at first I found it hard to warm up to him."[35] Dearden had scouted Joseph while he was auxiliary bishop in Atlanta, and decided that the young bishop was just the man he needed to guide the conference through a difficult period of transition. He lobbied Hallinan long and hard to release Joseph. It is not clear that Joseph was offered very much input into the decision, and Joseph always was frank about how long he resisted the move. Yet much as with Hallinan, Joseph and John Dearden grew to work together as a remarkably effective team. Joseph himself finally had to admit that leaving Atlanta to work at the conference "was the best thing that could ever have happened to me, and I am not speaking of appointments that I have received since then, but in terms of getting to know the church in this country and the universal church."[36] Joseph learned much from Dearden, a second mentor who molded and shaped him into the pastor he was becoming.

Joseph would eulogize Dearden many years later with strikingly similar words to those he used for Hallinan: "For the past twenty years our relationship has been a very close one. He was both a brother and a father to me. . . . He was my teacher and counselor. Above all, we were friends."[37] Yet, thinking also about the larger meaning of this period after the council with Hallinan and Dearden in Joseph's life, something else Joseph said about Dearden seems especially revealing. As much as Joseph was describing his mentor and friend, it is not difficult to imagine him talking about himself when he wrote that "the growth and renewal to which the council called the entire church also had a profound effect on the cardinal personally," and "He underwent a significant change as a result of his participation in the council."[38]

Joseph underwent that change, too. With Paul Hallinan and John Dearden, Joseph emerged changed from the council and the years immediately after it. The council transformed his view of the church and the flavor of his ministry. The years at the NCCB/USCC in Washington would place Joseph at the center of questions emerging from the council about what this new season in the Roman Catholic church would mean for administration, for liturgy, and for the role that the church would play in social and political life. Those issues never fell out of a central position in his ministry for the rest of his life, but they got their firm grounding in the years that Joseph spent working out the details of their application while he was general secretary of the conference. These years in Washington called upon and honed Joseph's intuitive skills as an administrator, giving him an instinctive grasp on how far and how quickly the church could move forward. Inevitably, for some the pace of progress was too quick just as for others it was too slow.

In the thrilling but challenging years after the council, the conference dealt with all sorts of difficulties with unauthorized, experimental liturgies while some grew impatient for more of the Latin to give way to contemporary languages.

At the same time, recalcitrant bishops in some dioceses refused to implement any of the changes in the liturgy, preferring to try to hold on to the old Latin Mass and everything that came with it. But that was not all. By 1969 warnings began to sound about a "grave crisis" in the priesthood as a large number of priests began to leave. The numbers became so overwhelming that by 1971 the Congregation for the Doctrine of the Faith adopted simplified procedures to laicize priests. As this crisis unfolded, the NCCB undertook a study of the American priesthood. Leaders of the study included Fr. Andrew Greeley, Fr. George Higgins, and Fr. Eugene Kennedy, all of whom would go on to play important roles in Joseph's life. Joseph played a difficult role during the study as the intermediary between some of the more traditional bishops and the research staff who were ready to ask any question, report any result. As Eugene Kennedy recalled those events, Joseph "was, in effect, mediating more than the priest study," but instead "was attempting to manage a major cultural change in ecclesiastical Catholicism."[39] The change could be seen in the survey results. Intended to help the bishops' conference address the crisis in the priesthood, the survey rather reported widely and publicly some surprising results that, in fact, did little to help the conference. To begin: "Conflicts with bishops and other authorities are seen as a greater source of frustration than" celibacy.[40] That hardly painted a happy picture of post-conciliar collegiality, a change in the way that bishops exercised their authority. The study all but announced to the world that local parish priests were dissatisfied with the pace of change after the council. There also were reports of priestly dissent to church teachings on contraception and divorce. The battle lines that would become so familiar inside the church in the decades following the council were forming in these years, and the priest survey confirmed that even priests were choosing sides as early as 1971. During these years, Joseph played for the first time a role he would continue to play until his last days. He sought, as Kennedy remembered those events, to bring people together over their differences. Joseph's basic instincts were toward conciliation and preserving the community of the church.

Joseph certainly did not prevent divisions from forming in the church in the years immediately after the council, but he did enjoy some significant successes during his years in Washington. Most of all Joseph succeeded finally to modernize the conference with new statutes for its organization. He began pushing for the revision of the conference statutes almost from his first days in Washington, and Rome gave final recognition to those revisions shortly before Joseph left Washington. Even today, the conference bears the double imprint of John Dearden and Joseph Bernardin, both of whom toiled through difficult years to make what today is called the United States Conference of Catholic Bishops what it is.

A final few things will illustrate Joseph's life and work during these years as a sensitive pastor working as an administrator to bring the church into the modern world. Joseph's ecumenical and interfaith work continued as he became part of an interfaith committee in 1968 that succeeded to lobby Congress to pass the Family Assistance Act in 1970. Building relationships outside the church, both in other faith communities as well as in American politics, had made it possible for Joseph to play a role in aiding poor families around the United States. But perhaps the most interesting episode is of comparatively small importance.

Joseph had come to know Frances Octavie Mosimann during his time in Charleston. Tanchie, as she was known only to an elect inner circle, grew up in a proud Charleston family and went to work for the diocese at a young age. She and Joseph worked together with remarkable effectiveness, and when the time came for Joseph to move to Washington, Tanchie accompanied him. Tanchie kept Joseph organized in a way up to his own exacting standards, and her help would be essential to help him succeed as general secretary of the bishops' conference. Tanchie was so important to Joseph's work life that she became "the first woman ever to attend the bishops' meetings, which had been closed to the public and only later were opened to the press." Tanchie described her presence at those meetings, taking notes at Joseph's direction, as "unprecedented," and remembered that "a few of the older bishops had some difficulty" with her being there.[41] It posed Joseph no difficulty. It seems as though he could have imagined no reason why Tanchie should not have been there.

Joseph's emerging character as a Catholic bishop formed by the Second Vatican Council was clear to see during these years in Washington, yet he frequently described how much he missed the pastoral work of being in a diocese, being near people, dealing with problems that affected women and men more directly. It should come as no surprise, then, that Joseph remembered the day in 1972 when he learned he was to become the archbishop of Cincinnati. Archbishop Luigi Raimondi, the apostolic delegate, gave Joseph the news and "asked me to go into his chapel and pray about it before accepting. 'No, archbishop,' I replied, 'I accept now. Then I'll go to the chapel and say a prayer of thanksgiving!' "[42]

Joseph would be a pastor after all.

CHAPTER THREE

From Cautious Bureaucrat to Pastor (1972–82)

Archbishop Joseph Bernardin did not become a good shepherd overnight.

A Cincinnati priest who knew Joseph remembered that when he arrived, he seemed only able to see problems in terms of the "big picture" and did not always think in terms of how decisions would affect ordinary Catholics.[1] Four years as the general secretary of the bishops' conference in Washington, two years as vicar general in Atlanta, and a fourteen-year apprenticeship to church administration in Charleston had conspired to keep Joseph almost entirely out of parishes, away from people. Joseph was a skilled administrator, and he had a peace-seeking personality borne out of childhood hardship and a family background shaped by the diversity of the Trento region. But he did not develop the skills of a pastor until he came to Cincinnati.

The years in Cincinnati were a necessary experience that prepared Joseph for his ministry in Chicago and for the worldwide stature he would achieve as both skilled churchman and beloved shepherd. But they would be difficult years. Joseph's time in Cincinnati would foreshadow events of the decades to come in the financial circumstances that would compel him to close and merge schools and parishes. More than that, Joseph would find himself at the center of controversy during a presidential election, on the spot in the US bishops' first struggle over the question of abortion in American national politics. Joseph would chair a bishops' committee that planned the Call to Action conference in 1976, a meeting of bishops and laypeople that ended in embarrassment for the bishops and division among American Catholics that still is with them today. In the midst of all of these tumultuous events, Joseph would experience a mid-life conversion and a revolution in his spiritual life. Cincinnati brought together all of the elements for which we remember Joseph Bernardin. In the words of one Cincinnatian who had observed Joseph closely, "something has happened to him in the past few years" while he was in Cincinnati. "He was a cautious bureaucrat who became a pastor."[2]

The bureaucratic task in Cincinnati must have seemed daunting to Joseph. In 1972 the Archdiocese of Cincinnati was home to nearly six hundred thousand Catholics, more than ten times as many Catholics as there were in Atlanta or in Charleston. In two years Joseph would have an auxiliary bishop, Daniel Pilarczyk. But in the early going, he was all on his own. Over the years leading up to Joseph's arrival, the archdiocese had seen considerable growth. Since the end of World War II, the archdiocese nearly had doubled. By the time of Joseph's installation, the growth had begun to reverse. Since the end of the war, Joseph's predecessors had built forty-four churches. In the twenty-five years following Joseph's installation, only ten new churches were built while a process of consolidating old parishes got underway.[3]

As went parishes, so went parish schools. Not six months after his installation in Cincinnati, Joseph would speak about the "serious difficulties" facing Catholic education and address the hard decisions about closing Catholic schools.[4] Before 1973 was over, Joseph would preside over the dedication of Chaminade-Julienne High School, one school merged from the consolidation of two, with characteristic optimism and humor, describing himself as the "presiding clergyman" at a marriage:

> Both schools have existed, under the names that we presently know them, since 1927. . . . Chaminade has been in pursuit of Julienne ever since Chaminade moved into the old red brick building that had been her home on this very site. . . . A forty-six year courtship may seem a very long one in human terms, but since the lives of institutions span much greater lengths of time than those of humans, perhaps it is not so long a time after all. . . . [Both schools] bring to this union a heritage and tradition that will make the union an unusually strong one, fruitful and enriching for the entire Dayton community.[5]

Joseph's cheerful description should not suggest that the consolidation was easy, or that he thought it would be. Joseph was clear in his understanding that it was "urgent . . . [to] adopt a positive attitude toward the future" in the light of new possibilities that those difficult changes made available. Like his openness to change and reform following the council, Joseph asked the people of Cincinnati to embrace the difficulties that accompanied the pain of seeing old parishes and old schools change or go away. The passage of time gives a "better understanding of the Church and its mission in today's world," and if we have the patience and courage to follow the path that is laid before us and to gain understanding from it, we can appreciate that "a consciousness of these problems is in itself a manifestation of life, a sign of hope."[6] The Spirit does not abandon us.

Against this backdrop of practical problems, Joseph conceived of his own role as bishop in the open spirit of the council. In his first meeting with the archdiocesan pastoral council, he spoke of the virtues of tension. Tension, he said, is a sign that everyone involved—priests, sisters, laypeople—really is saying what they mean, really talking to one another. Joseph invited that tension, even as he was cautious that "there should be little opportunity for conflict to develop."[7] This was the seasoned bureaucrat preparing the people of Cincinnati for the inevitable hard decisions that lay ahead, the experienced administrator who had navigated the stormy seas of conflict among the bishops at the conference in Washington. But this also was the open-minded peace seeker who saw opportunities in problems and no danger in openly expressing different points of view, so long as those discussions avoided personal conflict. Joseph had concluded his installation homily as archbishop of Cincinnati with the Prayer of Saint Francis. It was the first time publicly that Joseph would hint at his spiritual closeness to *il poverello*, the poor man of Assisi. Joseph's Franciscan spirituality would play a greater and greater role in his ministry over time. But early in Cincinnati, Joseph already had begun to shape his ministry into a channel of peace.

Perhaps it was somewhat unfair to call Joseph cautious. The years in Cincinnati were some of the most challenging years in recent American Catholic history. Barely two months after Joseph was installed as archbishop, the Supreme Court rendered its verdict in *Roe v. Wade*, effectively wiping away state laws that restricted access to abortion during the first three months of pregnancy. Joseph already was a highly visible figure in the American Catholic landscape—the day before the *Roe* decision was announced Joseph had preached at a White House ecumenical service. His response to the Supreme Court's decision would be watched closely both inside and outside the Catholic Church. To have assumed a national profile during such tumultuous years would chasten anyone, even someone so well prepared as Joseph. Years later his assistants would joke about his public statements, generated from the "Department of Nuance."[8] But the cautious nuance of Joseph's public statements surely was an expression of a personality that wanted to minimize conflict, bring people together, and treat issues carefully with respect for their full complexity.

If his public statements are any guide, the abortion decision certainly appears to have horrified Joseph in an unusual way. At least in the years immediately following *Roe v. Wade*, his public statements about it were among the least nuanced words ever associated with his name. In Joseph's 268-word statement following the announcement of the *Roe* decision, he described abortion as "evil" four times. It seems likely that several things were at the heart of what was, by the mild standard of Joseph Bernardin, a rather ferocious reaction to *Roe v. Wade*. Certainly there was the moral conviction that ending an innocent life is wrong. Beyond that, as a good and loyal churchman, Joseph must have been startled by the distance that suddenly had begun growing between American social life and longstanding, widely held convictions that transcended the differences among Catholics, Protestants, Jews, and all believers. Finally, it seems right to say that Joseph was perhaps even more alert to life's sacredness than many other people could be. Joseph had watched his father suffer through illness and had ministered to Paul Hallinan while he endured a long illness to his death. Joseph, who had wanted to study medicine before he wanted to become a priest, would have been especially sensitive about issues concerning human life. We can feel even surer to look at Joseph's response to the abortion issue this way, in the light of its unusual lack of nuance, because his subsequent public statements across several years struck the same tone.

In those earliest public statements about abortion, Joseph also gave some sign that he already was thinking in terms for which he would gain much more attention later. Two years after *Roe v. Wade*, Joseph observed: "Respect for life has dwindled considerably not only at the two extremes of life's spectrum but also in between. . . . If we are consistent, then, we must be concerned about life from beginning to end."[9] As early as 1975 Joseph had begun to think about a consistent ethic of life even as he struggled to find the right way to advance the issue in debates over public affairs. Again and again, Joseph strained against the idea that opposition to abortion was sectarian or somehow unique only to Catholics. Instead, Joseph insisted that the respecting the sacredness of life is a public value that does not depend on any religious affiliation. His frustrations mounted in a publicly visible way over just this question as Joseph dealt more and more with national politics as a church leader.

In 1974 the US bishops elected Joseph to be president of the NCCB/USCC. Only two years after leaving Washington as general secretary, Joseph would lead the American bishops in their conference and preside over the organization that he had done so much to mold and to shape. In the midst of the tumult in American politics following *Roe* and the disarray in the church following Pope Paul's encyclical letter that condemned contraception and the ongoing experimentation following the council, these would be difficult years in which to lead American Catholics. Joseph would face extraordinary tests. At moments those frustrations about the direction of American life would get the better of Joseph, lead him to places where he did not want to be. At the same time, we can see that Joseph never would have become the good pastor without these experiences.

As the years went by that saw *Roe* go unreversed and unmoderated, Joseph's statements on the topic remain equally, uncharacteristically exasperated. Joseph's concerns mounted through the mid-1970s as the debate over the right to life narrowed to focus on abortion alone. Joseph spoke in 1976 to that concern that there was more to the dignity of human life than merely protecting it before birth:

> Life before and after birth, from the moment of conception until death, is like a seamless garment. It all hangs together; one part cannot exist without the other. You cannot pick and choose. If we become insensitive to the beginning of life and condone abortion or if we become careless about the end of life and justify euthanasia, we have no reason to believe that there will be much respect for life in between. As a matter of fact, the evidence of history as well as the present moment leads us to the opposite conclusion.[10]

For Joseph, abortion sat at the center of the church's moral teachings that touch every aspect of human life. The depth of that commitment is revealed by how frequently he spoke about abortion as the foundation of a deep commitment to the sanctity of life. Joseph returned to the subject again and again in university addresses, in ecumenical contacts, and even in speeches to professional groups.

Joseph's attention fixed on these issues during the mid-1970s, and in many ways he never stopped trying to sort out how Americans can come together over a shared commitment to life. His earliest efforts were not always constructive and did not always go smoothly. When the Democratic Party adopted a platform plank opposing a constitutional amendment to overturn *Roe*, the NCCB/USCC launched into overdrive. Catholics and the Democratic Party had a long relationship that stretched through the Kennedy years of the 1960s all the way back to Al Smith, whom the Democrats made the first Catholic ever to be a major party nominee for president in 1928. Abortion threatened a serious rift in that longstanding relationship. Moreover, that long relationship should have meant it was more likely that Catholics would have better success getting support for the pro-life position from the Democrats. Governor Jimmy Carter, the Democratic nominee, was an evangelical Christian who was pro-life. But Carter was in a difficult position, too. He could not afford to alienate liberal voters by speaking up for a constitutional amendment that would overturn *Roe*.

During August of 1976, a series of discussions between the bishops' conference staff and representatives from the Carter campaign culminated in a meeting between the campaign and the bishops that included Gov. Carter and Joseph. It did not go well, and reporters waiting outside the meeting were eager to write about a breach between the bishops and the Democratic Party. Joseph's greatest concern, apart from the question of abortion, was to avoid putting the Catholic Church in the political spotlight, endorsing one candidate or another. Events quickly got beyond his or anyone else's control when the Republican Party adopted a platform more like what the bishops were hoping to see. President Ford invited Joseph and other members of the USCC to the White House for a meeting just ten days after the meeting with Carter and followed up with a five-page letter to Joseph stressing the many ways that the Republicans could further the church's social and political agenda. Quite without his intending it, and certainly not desiring it, Joseph's zeal for protecting innocent life had placed the church at the center of a political controversy as Republicans sought to court Catholic voters.

In fact, Joseph had already been worrying about the effects of the abortion issue a year earlier. In a 1975 speech to the convention of Serra International, Joseph spoke about the "polarization" that surrounded the church's efforts to find a place for its social justice commitments in American politics.[11] Even in the midst of the 1976 intrigue with the Carter campaign, Joseph urged "such action as would move the issue of a constitutional amendment from stage center because of the issue's potential for divisiveness."[12] Yet those divisions were taking root in the church and in American society, and there was little Joseph or anyone else could do to stop it. In many ways Joseph would spend the remainder of his life trying. But 1976 would not end without one further reminder of how difficult those divisions were.

As the United States neared its bicentennial year, all sorts of celebrations were planned. The bishops' conference sought to hold their own observance, and planning began in 1972. The bishops discussed a variety of ways to call attention to Catholic contributions to American life. Those included a prime time television special and a museum exhibit in Washington, DC. Dearden led a committee that studied many options and approved the final plans. Joseph was the committee's vice chair, and by 1973 Joseph had taken charge of the subcommittee for the conference on justice. Over the next three years, Joseph would plan and carry out an unprecedented, national meeting that included more than one hundred Catholic bishops and nearly three thousand laypeople. Typical of the careful planning Joseph brought to everything he did, the bishops would hear from more than eight hundred thousand people as they planned a conference agenda that took up subjects ranging from "Women in the Church" to "The Church and Divorced Catholics" to "Disarmament and Peace." Dearden spoke of the conference in terms of "the Bicentennial dialogue," an event that would pursue justice in the world as an objective by showing to the world the church as a model that would enliven justice, provide justice an opportunity to take "human shape" as the church "moves from living *with* people in society to *standing for* their needs and *speaking to* the wider society in the name of liberty and justice."[13] But the conference did not so much achieve those goals as it testified to the depth of differences within the church and illustrated the difficulty of bringing the social message of the Gospel to the wider world.

Before the conference was over, the delegates on the floor successfully passed motions that called for the ordination of women and the end of priestly celibacy, among several other things that the US bishops simply could not do. This bishops' conference and the opportunity for dialogue that the bishops had sought to create ended in an even deeper and more permanent division within the church. Not only can the lines between traditionalists and progressives that would become so familiar be traced to this Call to Action conference, but the outcome produced a sort of mutual suspicion and mistrust between laypeople and their bishops that had not existed before. In almost every way, the conference was a disaster for everyone involved, and it left Dearden and Joseph in difficult positions for having been so closely associated with it. Joseph observed, in a carefully nuanced statement, that "too much was attempted" and the meeting was "overwhelmed" by an expansive agenda. He promised that the recommendations would be evaluated and stressed above those promises that "together we must work for unity within the Church, a unity which is assured by the one Spirit who is present and at work in us all."[14] That certainly was as optimistic and conciliatory as any such statement could be. But perhaps Dearden later was able to say even more plainly what Joseph attempted to say with nuance:

> The results of the Bicentennial process may at this point seem hasty, untidy, careless, even extreme. But on closer examination, it seems to me that far more often the working papers and conference resolutions demonstrate a warmth and sympathy for the problems of church leadership on the part of our people, their enthusiastic affirmation of the Christian faith and hope, their sincere willingness to share in building a stronger church. No one expects us to endorse all that transpired in Detroit. People do expect us to continue the process by responding with decisive action where it is called for and with honest disagreement where it is necessary. The key to our actions in the future is to continue the process, to build on the hopes that have been awakened, to act upon our clear responsibility for the unity, fidelity and vision of the Catholic community.[15]

Some press accounts, particularly in the *New York Times* and in the *National Catholic Reporter*, suggested that Joseph and Dearden had emerged from the Call to Action meeting on opposite sides of how to move forward. Troubled by this, Joseph at one point wrote a rather personal letter to Dearden that began, "I feel badly about the publicity given to our Call-to-Action response," and went on to say that, "my only desire all along has been to get as much consensus as possible."[16] In fact, the record makes clear that

Joseph and Dearden agreed that the agenda of the conference had been too full, some of the resolutions had been extreme, and that there could be no acting on some of what the delegates called for inside the church. More important, the conference reflected a model of dialogue and community that Joseph and Dearden had been working to promote in the church since their time in Washington together began in 1968. And while perhaps both men lamented how the Call to Action conference ended, both remained resolute that the commitment to processes of dialogue was a more important achievement than anything the Call to Action delegates or the bishops hoped to achieve by the conference.

In all of these events that stretch from Dearden's vigorous efforts to recruit Joseph from Atlanta to the bishops' conference to the Call to Action meeting and beyond, we see the influence that Dearden had on Joseph. Dearden returned Joseph's friendship and affection. Eugene Kennedy recalled a story from the bishops' meeting that elected Joseph to be president of the bishops' conference, when "across the bishop filled room, Cardinal Dearden . . . smiled broadly as he said to a friend, 'Now, Joe can move!' "[17] These friends would remain close until Dearden's death in 1988, vacationing together and each trying to keep the spirit of dialogue alive inside the church. That commitment to dialogue was evidence of both men's ongoing conversion in the light of the council. Before Dearden had been appointed to Detroit, he was bishop of Pittsburgh from 1950 to 1958, where he was known as "Iron John," a "typical pre-Vatican man, armed with all kinds of rules and regulations which put fear into the hearts of many of his priests."[18] But the council had softened, changed the hardnosed "Iron John" into "Gentle John," someone who let others take on leadership and responsibility while he labored to make success possible for those around him.[19] Dearden's decentralization of the Archdiocese of Detroit and the aftermath of the Call to Action conference marked him as the leading liberal in the American church. People spoke of Dearden bishops long before they spoke of Bernardin bishops. But one thing all who described Dearden agreed about was that he was a "man of the church." As with Joseph, that description is essential to understand Dearden. The conversion that took place in Dearden was not a conversion that moved him from a conservative to a liberal. It only was a conversion in how he understood the church. Through the council, Dearden came to understand that "the mystery of the Church lives in the entire people of God."[20] The changes in how this man of the church undertook his ministry followed from this basic insight. Never straying from his loyalty to the church, and only changing in his understanding of what the church was, Dearden must have recognized a kindred soul and a partner in Joseph who, though younger, had undergone something like a similar conversion while remaining in all a man of the church.

Alongside controversy, ongoing conversion was a theme of these years in Joseph's life. While living in Washington at the bishops' conference, Joseph began visiting the Franciscan Monastery of the Holy Land on Quincy Street. He developed a close relationship to the friars, hearing their confessions as sometimes they heard his. It is not difficult to imagine a Franciscan spirituality at work in Joseph even before he drew close to the friars in Washington. Signs could be found in the peace pastoral he cosigned with Hallinan, in his peace seeking over differences of race or politics or faith, and, in his conciliating personality. Joseph journeyed to Assisi in 1975 during one of his frequent trips to Rome as president of the bishops' conference. He began an extraordinary "Homily on St. Francis" with the shocking news that "I am a Franciscan too! Several years ago, the Franciscans honored me by receiving me into their first order and investing me with the Franciscan habit."[21]

Indeed, that was true. The Holy Name Province of the Order of Friars Minor, the Franciscans, received Joseph into their first order in May 1972.[22] Joseph seemed to take this Franciscan association quite seriously and always made an effort to divert to Assisi when he was in Italy and his schedule could permit it. But his formal affiliation with the Franciscans was something he discussed infrequently, usually with the effect of puzzling the people around him. Years later, one of his priest assistants in Chicago recalled Joseph saying that it was possible to "be diocesan and Franciscan at the same time," while another recalled a conversation weeks before Joseph died when he described how much he really wanted to be buried in the Franciscan habit.[23] The Franciscan theme would continue throughout Joseph's ministry, peace building and reconciliation taking on even greater importance for him as years passed. In his funeral homily for Cardinal Bernardin, Msgr. Kenneth Velo recalled that Joseph always kept the Prayer of St. Francis in his pocket, with him. To understand the depth of St. Francis's importance for Joseph, the best testimony can be found in that 1975 homily Joseph gave in Assisi:

> The thing we need most in our highly secularized and sophisticated world is the *spirit* of St. Francis. What kind of spirit is this? It is a spirit that puts God in the very center of life. . . . It is a spirit that derives a great deal of joy from the simple things of life. . . . It is a spirit that prompts us to love our neighbor. . . . Finally, it is a spirit that prompts us to be truthful, open persons of integrity at all times; to approach life with a simplicity that frequently we see only in small children. . . . When this is done, not only

do we reconcile ourselves with God, but we also reconcile ourselves with our brothers and sisters.[24]

In the controversies he faced back home in the United States about abortion, and the increasing divisions that dominated American life and the church, Joseph saw a path toward reconciliation through simplicity and a renewed spiritual commitment. In great tumult, Joseph turned even more fully toward the way of peace.

During these years, and with these Franciscan themes fixed in his imagination, the mid-1970s were a time that found Joseph thinking more and more deeply about prayer, especially his own prayer life. When Archbishop James J. Byrne invited Joseph to offer a series of talks at the Institute of Spirituality in Saint Paul, Minnesota, in 1974, Joseph took the opportunity to develop his thoughts on prayer in a way that clearly stayed with him for the remainder of his life. Not surprisingly, Joseph cast a renewed commitment to prayer in terms of fulfilling the hopes of the Second Vatican Council. He said that "no renewal is worthy of the name unless it flows from a change in mind and heart; unless it is first and foremost a renewal of spirit."[25] Joseph argued for the importance of seeing prayer as "not just 'one more thing' in our lives," and saying instead, "It is everything. It is the basic expression and nutrient of our faith."[26] He also told a personal story:

> The absolute necessity of making time for prayer, whether liturgical or private, came home very forcefully to me a few weeks ago. My schedule is unbelievable. I simply did not have the time to do more than celebrate Mass and pray a small part of the Breviary for several days in a row. Suddenly it dawned on me: 'My life for many years to come will probably be as busy as it has been for the past several

days. Therefore, I may never have time to pray adequately again.' Immediately I saw the ridiculousness of the situation and determined, once again, to give prayer a real priority in my life.[27]

This was, perhaps, a different version of the story that Joseph related later in *The Gift of Peace*. He described a dinner in the mid-1970s with two young priests he had ordained since arriving in Cincinnati. He told them of the difficulty he had finding time to pray, and he asked for their help. Surprisingly, they challenged him to make a change. Perhaps even more surprisingly, the archbishop of Cincinnati listened and heeded their urgings. Joseph talked about that event many times throughout the rest of his life and described it as a turning point in *The Gift of Peace*. Recognizing what those priests were telling him as raising a question about his effectiveness as a priest and bishop, as well as raising a question about integrity and sincerity, Joseph acted on the advice of those young priests, and he continued until his final illness prevented him from praying. From that time on Joseph recalled, "I decided to give God the first hour of my day, no matter what, to be with him in prayer and meditation." And he did. Each day, he would spend the first hour alone in quiet prayer, and he was realistic enough about prayer to know that being in the Lord's presence was enough, "whether I'm actually praying, daydreaming or dozing off!"[28] The value was not in a particular activity, but in giving the time to God. Monsignor Kenneth Velo, who lived with Joseph in the archbishop's residence in Chicago, recalled that Joseph continued this discipline of prayer until the end of his life, for as long as he had the strength to do it.

The importance of that turning point in Joseph's life would be difficult to overestimate. Yet, we should notice that it was only one more episode in a lifelong sequence of spiritual awakenings in Joseph's life. Joseph, himself, said that "once again" in the mid-1970s he had decided to give "priority" to his prayer life. He had had difficulty in his prayer life before. In a very personal series of retreat talks he gave for priests later on in Chicago, Joseph recalled the journey toward the renewal of his prayer life and his faith. He recalled a dinner with an older priest in South Carolina, shortly after his own ordination. This older priest described a priest he knew as a "good Catholic."

Joseph laughed. "Certainly, if he was a priest, he was a good Catholic!"

The older priest told him, "Not necessarily. This man is a real believer. He takes the sacraments seriously in his personal life."[29]

Young Joseph, only twenty-five, didn't know it then. But that older priest's observation would come back to him not many years later. Joseph told the priests of Chicago:

> I was a young, busy priest—running from one thing to another. . . . Then one day I had a crisis of faith. I suddenly felt that I really didn't believe Jesus was present in the sacraments I was administering, including the Eucharist. He wasn't really present in the sacramental and non-sacramental encounters I was having with people. I was bewildered, frightened. Everything in my ministry became "make believe." I felt alone, abandoned, worth very little. I seriously thought that I should leave and probably would have, if leaving active ministry had been more "acceptable" at the time. Fortunately, I had the good sense to talk with a close priest friend who encouraged me to make a retreat. During that retreat, in desperation, I cried out for help and the Lord answered! Suddenly everything came back into focus. If he doesn't feed me, I starve. If I don't accept his

sustenance, I wither away. It was a very scary experience,
but it taught me a valuable lesson.[30]

Joseph would need to relearn that lesson again in the
mid-1970s, and he would struggle to maintain the discipline
to pray throughout his life. The message that comes from
these experiences is one that would be familiar to the spiritual masters, from John of the Cross, to Thomas Merton,
or to anyone who had read them. The spiritual life is an
ongoing struggle—indeed, "A struggle with prayer may be
a sign of a vibrant relationship" with Jesus.[31] We will sometimes retreat and withdraw from that relationship. "Maybe
we are afraid to be a friend to Jesus because we know that
friends ask much more than strangers do. We sense that he
will ask too much, or seek greater intimacy than we can
bear. We are frightened."[32] It takes an effort to return to the
relationship, to maintain it, and keep it living and growing.
Joseph knew this part of the spiritual life well.

Those audiences at retreat talks he gave on prayer and
the spiritual life were priests. Joseph also offered his long
experience of the spiritual life and all he learned in a pastoral reflection for the people of the Archdiocese of Chicago.
"Christ Lives in Me" appeared in 1985, and with that document Joseph made his witness to the spiritual life a part of
his public ministry as a Catholic bishop. Again, themes of
conversion and self-understanding sound clearly in "Christ
Lives in Me." Those themes merge in Joseph's observation
that "to experience true conversion, we must first honestly
face our innermost self which exists independently of external circumstances and pressures."[33] Joseph's hard-won life
of prayer emerged from the crucible of his difficult experiences as a young, busy priest, as archbishop in Cincinnati,
and as president of the bishops' conference during years of

turmoil and trouble, to offer something unique and his own to the people of Chicago, his flock as their bishop, and to people everywhere. The clarity and insight that Joseph had obtained through prayer became something he was eager to share, not only as a matter of giving that gift of prayer and peace to Catholics in his archdiocese, but also as a means to bring that peace to the world. Joseph spoke of prayer as something that frustrates our tendency to "dichotomize" or "to separate and break apart elements which are in fact unities."[34] Prayer, when we are attentive to it, compels us to see past false divisions, and that seeing can become a source of peace for us and among us because we learn to unmask "false dichotomies." Those false dichotomies can be found outside the church in social and political life. Joseph spoke of false dichotomies "between the individual and the institution," "between pluralism and unity," and "between the sacred and the secular," and he would spend the rest of his public ministry in efforts to overcome them all.[35] But the root of that ministry and Joseph's insights into the falseness of these divisions was, and always remained, prayer.

In a way that seems more surprising looking back than it did in the 1970s, Joseph shared these insights with another bishop shaped by the Second Vatican Council, someone whose influence would shape the rest of his life. As the archbishop of Cincinnati, Joseph was shepherd to one of the largest Polish populations in the United States. It only was natural that Joseph should visit Poland during his time in Cincinnati and, for the archbishop of Krakow, having the president of the American bishops' conference visit his Soviet-dominated homeland was a major event. Joseph and Cardinal Karol Wojtyła got to know each other well during that 1976 trip. As years went by, Joseph's reputation as a church liberal might appear to make a good relationship with the conservative Pope John Paul II seem improbable. But to see it that way would be just another false dichotomy. Both men had been transformed by the council, a key event in their lives, and both men also understood the need for a "new apologetics" and a renewed focus on "evangelization," both terms that Pope John Paul would popularize in the 1980s while Joseph had been talking about them during the 1970s. In 1987 Pope John Paul would come to visit Joseph's South Carolina hometown and the parish where he was baptized, and, though it may be more difficult to appreciate since Pope Francis has become known for phoning people, Joseph was moved to speechlessness when Pope John Paul phoned him in his office in 1993 after Steven Cook recanted his false allegation of sexual misconduct against Joseph.

Of course, Wojtyła went to Rome in 1978, and only four years later Joseph would leave Cincinnati for Chicago. The understanding between those two men formed the foundation for Joseph's place over the next ten years as the most influential American churchman. Joseph never would have ended up in Chicago if it had not been for his relationship with the pope. An intrigue erupted in the last year of Cardinal John Cody's life, and it very nearly ruined Joseph's reputation. Cody had been the archbishop of Chicago since 1965, and his ministry had been tumultuous. As Cody's life neared its end, a reporter publicized the fantastic musings of a Chicago priest who had hoped to get Joseph installed as Chicago's next archbishop and to use his relationship with Joseph to influence the church in the United States and in Rome. The most troubling implication of these accounts was that Joseph was complicit in the scheme. Perhaps Pope John Paul, knowing Joseph as he did, simply could not believe the accounts. In any event, he called Joseph to Rome in early

July 1982. Whatever the two men discussed, it is clear that the question of Joseph's motives or involvement with such a strange plot was put to rest. Days later the Holy See announced Joseph to be the next archbishop of Chicago. Pope John Paul's trust and confidence in Joseph was undisturbed.

Perhaps the relationship between Joseph and Pope John Paul II, and how it should upset the temptation to give in to dichotomies, is the most important thing to focus on during these years in Joseph's life. The time in Cincinnati was not only a time of transition from "a cautious bureaucrat" to "a pastor" but also were years when Joseph brought into focus the perspective for which he would come to be known. The consistent ethic of life was born from these years of *Roe v. Wade* and the 1976 election, as much as the Common Ground Initiative came from a determination to undercut the "false dichotomies" that too often cloud our perspective. In all these things, the foundation in prayer and a personal relationship with Jesus cannot be separated, and Joseph's own spiritual renewal is also a part of the story of his ministry to Cincinnati.

In these ways and in more, Joseph's Cincinnati ministry was essential to his growth as a bishop and as a shepherd, a distinction worth drawing. A Catholic bishop plays three roles. He is a teacher of the faith, he is an administrator who governs, and he is a spiritual leader who sanctifies the people of God. Many bishops excel at one or maybe two of those roles. The ones who succeed in all three roles are rare. Joseph came to the priesthood with the gifts of an administrator, and his early priesthood and time as a bishop in Atlanta and in Washington honed those skills to excellence. While working with Paul Hallinan in Atlanta, Joseph began his ministry as a teacher of the faith in the pastoral letter on war and peace. Yet it was his time in Cincinnati and as president of the bishops' conference that compelled him again and again to present the Catholic faith to those inside and outside the church on issues like abortion and the pace of reform after the council. Finally, it was the revolution in Joseph's personal prayer life that focused his administrative gifts and teaching skill toward the pastoral good of souls. A bishop is one who is consecrated to the work of the church and who has authority to govern, to teach, and to sanctify. But a shepherd, a pastor of souls, is one whose leadership in those roles is recognized and acclaimed by the people of God. Joseph went from a cautious bureaucrat to a pastor, from a bishop to a shepherd, during his time in Cincinnati.

During these years while that transition was underway, Joseph also had become one of the most visible bishops in the United States. Of course, that was at least partly due to the fact that he was president of the bishops' conference during these years. Then again, Joseph only became president of the conference because of the extraordinary confidence placed in him at a young age by his fellow bishops. His public visibility contributed to the crisis of the mid-1970s that brought about the transformation of his prayer life, and it changed his life in other ways, too. During his ministry in Cincinnati, Joseph preached or gave speeches throughout the United States and around the world, usually by invitation, traveling to fourteen states outside the immediate region of southern Ohio and visiting five countries.

For Joseph, to be a Catholic bishop was to approach the people of God, their joys, their hopes, their griefs, and their sorrows with an open heart and open ears. Most emphatically, his understanding of being a bishop did not include playing it safe. Even as his public profile soared to higher levels throughout the 1970s on the national and international stages, Joseph did not avoid difficult or controversial topics. In 1979 Joseph began to preach at special Masses in Cincinnati for separated and divorced Catholics, a ministry he brought with him to Chicago. Catholics in these sad circumstances pose a special challenge for the church's sacramental theology, and the best theological minds have not found an ideal way to treat the problem. Joseph saw people in need of comfort, and he reached out to them from within the church to tell them that the church was with them, and that he, a bishop of the church, came to them "as a loving, caring brother who wants to . . . identify himself with you so that he can be your strength and your support."[36]

Joseph's intense interest in the renewal of his own prayer life and prayer within the church led him to take an interest in the charismatic renewal during the 1970s. He preached at many of their events, lending them his support and prestige at a time when his fellow bishops derided the charismatic gatherings as "séances." But whatever we say about the charismatic renewal, we must at least say that Joseph encouraged them, believed that there could and should be space inside the church to try something that was new, and that may indeed be a movement of the Spirit.

Finally, it was while he was in Cincinnati that Joseph took on an interest in dialogue with the Jewish community. The Catholic Church has had a difficult relationship with Judaism throughout the centuries. There are many bridges that need to be rebuilt, even today. The twentieth century was a painful one, especially for the relationship between Catholics and Jews. The Second Vatican Council had taken special note of this problem, and Joseph was ever sensitive to the teachings of the council. He spoke as a guest of many Jewish groups while in Cincinnati and was recognized by the Jewish community with awards for the depth of his commitment to interreligious dialogue. This work would continue in Chicago, and his funeral would be the scene of the first Jewish prayer service for a Catholic archbishop that anyone could remember taking place inside a cathedral. That close relationship to the Jewish community began at a temple service in Cincinnati, where Joseph recalled this story about Pope John: "A short time after his election, Pope John received a group of Jews in audience. In a very spontaneous way, to show his love and respect for his guests, the Holy Father opened his arms wide and greeted them with these words: 'I am your brother, Joseph.' I wish this evening to use that same greeting. I too am your brother, Joseph."[37] Of course, Joseph would use the greeting again. It was only natural, and not just because of the inspiration he drew from Good Pope John. Joseph Bernardin would toil in a land far from his home for many years. He would labor in the arid landscape of postwar American culture to cultivate a remnant that could nourish the souls of believers. And, ever mindful of his brothers' tendency to quarrel (Gen 45:24), Joseph never ceased to be an ardent peacemaker outside and inside the church.

The final decade and a half of his ministry would make clear how deep the connection ran between Joseph and his scriptural namesakes, even as that time would test his spiritual commitments as much as any biblical prophet was tested. Hard, great days lay ahead as Joseph left Cincinnati. Cincinnati, Washington, Atlanta, and Charleston all had prepared Joseph to face them.

CHAPTER FOUR

"I Am Joseph, Your Brother"
(1982–93)

Cardinal John Cody had been archbishop of Chicago since 1965. Born in Saint Louis, he came to Chicago by way of New Orleans, where he had assisted Archbishop Joseph Rummel. Both Cody and Rummel publicly and courageously opposed segregation in mid-century Louisiana as much as Hallinan and Bernardin had done it in Georgia and South Carolina. Cody brought that commitment to civil rights with him to Chicago, and no mention of Cody should fail to credit his commitment to racial justice in a city so segregated that many people at the time described Chicago as "up South." Cody's years in Chicago were difficult for many reasons. But Cody did not make them any easier for himself.

At the time of Cody's death in 1982, federal prosecutors were investigating him for financial improprieties and salacious rumors circulated about his relationship with a woman. It is said that, before Pope Paul VI died, he was weighing whether to remove Cody, and that John Paul II had hoped to transfer him to a Vatican office. Perhaps worse than anything else about Cody's time in Chicago was his relationship with priests. The assessments even of a scholarly treatment sponsored by the Archdiocese of Chicago reflect the depth of the problem:

> Journalists compared [Cody] to the insecure Captain Queeg in the novel *The Caine Mutiny*. Queeg was so obsessed with who stole strawberries that he neglected his duty and never noticed the growing mutiny on his ship. So too, Cody immersed himself in trivial details, often letting more important matters pile up and ignoring the disaffection of his clergy. The subordinates with whom Cody surrounded himself tended to be yes-men, cronies, or soulless bureaucrats . . . . Even when these subordinates made the right decisions, the manner in which they acted lost respect for the archdiocese.[1]

When Joseph arrived in Chicago to be Cody's successor, he had his work cut out for him. Chicago needed a peacemaker in so many ways, and it was on that note Joseph began his ministry. He told the priests, "I think you are a remarkable group of men. I praise you and applaud you. It is a privilege and a challenge to be called to serve as head of the presbyterate in this archdiocese. I count on your help in meeting the challenges that lie before us."[2]

In his remarkable introduction to the priests and the archdiocese, Joseph offered a personal history that echoed things he had said on leaving Cincinnati just weeks earlier. At a critical moment in his life, this transition from a dauntingly large pastoral challenge in Cincinnati to an even greater one in Chicago, Joseph could look back with equanimity to see the steps that had prepared the way for him. Leaving Cincinnati, Joseph recalled the "many wonderful things" that had happened to him there, including how he "had changed since coming" to Cincinnati, how he had learned to focus "more on Christ Jesus and less on myself and those things that distract us from the Lord."[3] Arriving in Chicago, he recalled the influence of Hallinan and Dearden as "two of the most influential priests in my life," and he reflected on how "The priests of Cincinnati were especially helpful to my spiritual growth. . . . Theirs was a wonderful and permanent gift."[4] For the priests of Chicago, these words were a balm for the wounds of the last several years. They carried the promise of a new era in Chicago, one focused on robust implementation of the Second Vatican Council.

For many years Chicago had been an important local church in the United States. The city of Chicago had been incorporated only in 1837, ravaged by fire in 1871 and again in 1874. Yet its geographical position as a railroad hub fixed on major waterways made it a natural center of industry and an attractive destination for the flood of immigrants pouring into the United States during the late-nineteenth century, searching for employment and a better life. From the first fire in 1871 until Chicago's establishment as an archdiocese in 1908, the city's population more than quadrupled, quickly making Chicago a home to more than two million people. Those immigrants coming to Chicago were overwhelmingly Catholic, and that great growth quickly made Chicago into a place that Rome could not ignore. Fewer than one hundred years after the founding of the city, George Mundelein became Chicago's first cardinal-archbishop in 1924. By 1983 Joseph would be the archdiocese's fifth cardinal-archbishop.

Surprising only because it came so quickly, Pope John Paul II named Joseph to the College of Cardinals just six months after his installation as archbishop. Not only the size and stature of the Chicago archdiocese seemed to assure Joseph's cardinalate, but his leadership within the church made it inevitable. Still, to have been named cardinal so soon after coming to Chicago was an undeniable sign of the pope's confidence in Joseph, his desire that Joseph should be a leading voice in American Catholicism. More than that, Joseph's quick elevation to the College of Cardinals assured that he would be able to act on his commitments to the council.

Since the time of Cardinal Mundelein, Chicago had been a vital center of new thinking in the American church. Mundelein brought the 28th International Eucharistic Congress to Chicago in 1926, the first time such an event came to the United States. Mundelein also appointed the legendary Reynold Hillenbrand to be rector of Chicago's St. Mary of the Lake Major Seminary. Hillenbrand, a follower of Joseph Cardijn's model of specialized Catholic action, shaped a generation of Chicago priests whose social and church activism made Chicago the American archdiocese that had the greatest impact on liturgy and worship in the United States through its Office for Divine Worship. In other words, Chicago was an archdiocese well prepared by its history to receive Joseph, an archbishop so much shaped by the council. After seventeen years with Cody, Chicago was simply thirsty for an archbishop who would implement the council's directives not only with faithfulness but with cheerful enthusiasm.

Joseph recalled some of that history in his first pastoral letter as archbishop of Chicago, Our Communion, Our Peace, Our Promise, where he wrote: "The church in Chicago is known throughout the United States and even beyond for its liturgical leadership which began long before Vatican II."[5] The subject Joseph chose for that first pastoral letter, and the way in which he treated the subject, expresses the comfortable fit between Joseph and the Archdiocese of Chicago in terms of communion, peace, and promise. Joseph, characteristically, begins the letter with thanks. He is grateful not only for the prominent leadership the archdiocese has shown in the United States and around the world, but for the less visible role that so many people throughout Chicago play in bringing the liturgy to life. He is grateful to lectors, ministers of music, altar servers, and even to the people in the pews who worship week after week. Gratitude runs like a thread throughout the letter, but so does the implicit connection between liturgy and life, "our communion" and "our peace," that characterized how the council described the liturgy, and how Joseph had approached it for so long. Liturgy "is not passive—it is something we *do*," Joseph reminds us, recalling the ancient sense of liturgy being "the people's work" (*leitourgia* in Greek) that the council recovered in its Constitution on the Sacred Liturgy. He also reminds us that we depart the Mass "as a holy people always in mission"—"The spirit which fills us in the liturgy inspires us to re-create the world and doing so to prepare ourselves for fulfillment in heaven."[6]

Announcing himself to be in sympathy with the history and the people of Chicago, Joseph came as archbishop to be a peacemaker. It was a role he had played in Washington, in Atlanta, and even in Charleston. Yet now, secure in the confidence he enjoyed from his people in Chicago, from his fellow bishops, and from Pope John Paul, Joseph could feel free to take his peacemaking a giant step further, even while changing nothing fundamentally about it at all. The connection between Christian life and living in the world had been clear in the pastoral letter on the Vietnam War that Joseph had signed with Archbishop Hallinan, and it had been a part of his decades-long interaction with civil rights questions. Throughout the 1970s, during his lengthy political engagement with the abortion question, Joseph reflected for a long time on the interrelatedness of all of the issues affecting human life. Quickly after he arrived in Chicago, that long reflection bore fruits that would endure long after Joseph's death.

Work had begun in the bishops' conference to write a pastoral letter for the nation about the nuclear arms race years before Joseph was appointed to be archbishop of Chicago. In part, The Challenge of Peace was born from the difficult experience Joseph had during the 1976 presidential election. After the imbroglio that followed the meetings with Carter and Ford in 1976, Joseph became "convinced" that "the conference had to establish its own forum for its collective deliberation on current moral and ethical issues."[7] Rather than play by the rules that serve reporters and politicians, feeding scandal and division instead of providing guidance or illumination, Joseph hoped to use the collegial procedures of the conference to teach the Catholic faith in social life in a more sober, careful, and deliberative way. At the same time, working in the conference posed its own problems. Like American society and the whole church, the bishops' conference was full of men who saw questions of war and peace differently. When building the committee that would write the pastoral letter, Joseph was mindful of the problems and, rather than avoid them, faced them head on, inviting every point of view into the process. Joseph's committee to write the pastoral letter included Thomas Gumbleton, a Detroit auxiliary bishop and a peace activist as well as John O'Connor, bishop of Scranton who retired from the Navy as a rear admiral in the chaplain corps and later became cardinal-archbishop of New York. As Joseph saw the matter, "unless we fight it out in the committee, unless we reach some consensus there, we will never get the consensus."[8]

The bishops' *ad hoc* committee began meeting to find that consensus in 1980. It may be difficult to remember so many years later, but the early 1980s were dominated by nuclear fear that had not gripped the world in quite the same way since the Cuban missile crisis in 1962. Ronald Reagan had been elected president of the United States in 1980 on a promise of restoring American military power and renewed confrontation with the Soviet Union. By 1983 the nuclear stakes of those promises had become clear to everyone, especially for a generation of Americans who could remember the missile crisis of 1962, which included every Catholic bishop in the United States. The growing nuclear threat in the early 1980s posed an immediate moral problem. Yet, sorting out that moral problem was far from easy. Since ancient times, the church has taught that Christians may resort to violence in self-defense, a key consideration in the doctrine of the just war. In the 1980s, the question was whether a deterrent nuclear arms stockpile that led to a nuclear arms race (each nation seeking to possess more nuclear weapons than the other) qualified as legitimate self-defense.

The Challenge of Peace faced these questions directly. On the question of deterrence, the bishops wrote bluntly that "the quest for nuclear superiority must be rejected," and that, if it is legitimate at all, "deterrence should be used as a step on the way toward progressive disarmament" (188). The bishops' pastoral letter on war and peace did not duck the larger issue, either. The bishops expressed "profound skepticism about the moral acceptability of any use of nuclear weapons," adding that, "It would be a perverted political policy or moral casuistry which tried to justify using a weapon which 'indirectly' or 'unintentionally' killed a million innocent people because they happened to live near a 'militarily significant target' " (193). Those were tough words in 1983, yet they were backed up by a firm consensus among the bishops who approved them by a vote of 195–71, as well as by an extraordinary depth of research. The firmness of that consensus faced the most withering pressure, as the Reagan administration suggested that the bishops were naïve, deluded, and in over their heads so far as to have become "unwitting agents of the Kremlin."[9] William P. Clark, Jr., President Reagan's national security advisor and a Catholic, challenged the bishops in a letter published by the *New York Times*, asserting that the United States could not negotiate for a nuclear freeze, and that any agreement with the Soviets would demand that, "our deterrent forces remain sufficiently strong and credible to assure effective deterrence."[10] The bishops and the administration could not have been farther apart.

Joseph kept a cool head throughout the controversy. He observed, simply, that "it is inevitable when you discuss matters of this kind . . . there is going to be a great deal of feeling," and "it makes the process a little more interesting." It was not the first time he found himself in the middle of a national political storm. Yet, his calm detachment over the problem probably had another inspiration, too. Joseph was aiming at something larger than the nuclear issue as he led the bishops to consensus in The Challenge of Peace. Since 1976 Joseph had been speaking about continuity among all of the issues implicating human life in terms of a "seamless garment." From his experience in the late 1970s and all of the attention focused on abortion, Joseph understood the need to connect questions of war and peace to questions about abortion and euthanasia. Working on The Challenge of Peace from 1980–1983 provided a culminating experience for Joseph in his defining contribution to the Catholic moral perspective, which he delivered in a Fordham University lecture only seven months after the bishops' conference released the pastoral letter on the nuclear arms race.

Joseph made the connection between those experiences as he introduced his Gannon Lecture at Fordham on December

6, 1983. Joseph described his intention to address The Challenge of Peace in "a very specific manner," and described the pastoral letter as "a starting point for shaping a consistent ethic of life in our culture."[11] Joseph developed the language of "a consistent ethic of life" as a clearer way to talk about seeing "our opposition to abortion and our opposition to nuclear war . . . as specific applications of this broader attitude," an attitude that would recognize "the sanctity of life . . . from womb to tomb."[12] His idea was to overcome the distinctions drawn in political life between the protection of innocent human life in different circumstances, and to set the whole conversation into a context of "a broader attitude in society about respect for human life."[13]

Joseph repeated the metaphor of "a seamless garment" to describe his purpose, a phrase he had used first in 1976. This bit of imagery draws from John 19, which refers to Psalm 22. The gospel tells of Jesus' cloak that the soldiers divided before the crucifixion: "They took his clothes and divided them into four parts, one for each soldier. They also took his tunic; but the tunic was seamless, woven in one piece from the top" (v. 23). As a metaphor, the seamless garment identified Joseph's purposes closely with the person of Jesus. That metaphor emphasized the unbreakable unity among questions pertaining to human life, whether talking about abortion, war, the death penalty, economic justice, or anything else. Yet, over time, the substitution of "a seamless garment" for "a consistent ethic of life" fostered gross misunderstandings of what Joseph was trying to do. Some of the most prominent Catholic bishops in the United States charged Joseph with promoting a false equivalence among those issues. Abortion was the murder of innocents, they said. It was different from other issues and qualitatively more serious. New York's Cardinal John O'Connor said, "If the unborn in a mother's womb is unsafe it becomes ludicrous for the bishops to address the threat of nuclear war."[14] Boston's Cardinal Bernard Law emphasized abortion as the "key political issue" while coolly countenancing nuclear war as "a future possibility."[15] These bishops would not accept any equivalence between abortion and other issues.

Of course, Joseph was not arguing equivalence. As months and years unfolded after the Gannon Lecture, he continued to refine the argument for the consistent ethic and to clarify his meaning to soothe the worries of his critics. He said, "There are distinguishing differences between abortion and war," but that while "the *differences* among these cases are universally acknowledged; a consistent ethic seeks to highlight the fact that differences do not destroy the elements of a *common moral challenge*."[16] Joseph hoped to offer a theological reply to the consuming challenge of modern life. Our technological progress has made fantastic changes to the way we live, but technology also has isolated us from one another. Technology poses challenges to our communities and to our persons. Locked in our safe homes watching our televisions, we spend less time with our neighbors. Advancements in medical science made it possible to have a safe abortion, to raise new questions about life's ending, or to kill untold numbers of civilians in a war. At the root of all of these changes lies something more important, the way that they all reduce persons to less than what they are. War victims are statistics. The unborn baby is a fetus. We stop seeing one another for who and what we are, each a full human being who was created and is loved by God. We start seeing one another as problems to be solved, and technology provides solutions. Joseph had been sensitive to this growing problem throughout his priestly career, and the consistent ethic was the summation of his thoughtful engagement with it. He was alert to the complexity, the distinctiveness of each moral situation. Yet, Joseph was wise to see that solving the problem of abortion or any other, individual problem would not be enough to solve the deeper problem. Even today, we are in danger of losing sight of how truly wonderful each human being is.

Joseph could not have foreseen and certainly did not intend that the consistent ethic should become a point of division within the church. In retrospect, it still is difficult to imagine how it did. Perhaps the answer could be that the divisions already existed, and unwittingly Joseph provided a means for those divisions to break out. Still, as a reconciler by nature, Joseph never stopped trying to heal those divisions in the church. That effort would continue for the rest of his life.

At the same time, difficult problems in Chicago also challenged Joseph's desire to be a source of unity. The clergy sex abuse crisis had simmered at a low boil for decades around the United States, and it would not become the infamy that still beleaguers the church today until six years after Joseph's death. Throughout the twentieth century, the church largely dealt with priest pedophilia as a moral defect. Like its slowness to recognize modern science in other ways, the church was slow to embrace a psychological understanding of this disorder. Until very recently, such things were treated as sins against chastity that only required penance. Even after church leaders turned to treatment for abusive priests, there were overly optimistic expectations for a cure and almost never were allegations disclosed to parishioners or law enforcement authorities.

During his earliest years in Chicago, Joseph also followed the familiar pattern and transferred priests from one parish to another after an allegation of misconduct. Things changed after an allegation made at a suburban parish in 1991 blossomed into a city-wide scandal. Typical of his style, Joseph opened a process of dialogue with the parishioners, explaining so far as it was possible why their pastor was removed from ministry. Through that dialogue, the people became aware that there had been previous accusations against the priest in other parish assignments, and they were outraged. In response, Joseph formed a special commission to study how the Archdiocese of Chicago handled allegations of misconduct, and by the time that commission made its report a year later the archdiocese already had removed from active ministry twenty-two priests against whom accusations had been made. When that commission made its report, and once Joseph swiftly implemented the recommendations, Chicago became the first Catholic archdiocese in the United States to require the reporting of every allegation to law enforcement officials.

There can be no getting around the fact that Joseph did what every other bishop in the United States did about clerical sex abuse for many years. For a time, things were no better in Chicago than anywhere else. As we think about Joseph's role in the crisis, however, that fact cuts both ways. Certainly, Joseph was captive to the same way of looking at the problem that had dominated the whole church for decades. On the other hand, he changed his mind and moved the archdiocese into a radically different direction. Joseph was the first prominent churchman in the United States to step forward and try to change how the church dealt with sexual abuse. Chicago, under Joseph's leadership, was nearly the first diocese in the United States to take on the problem more seriously, in a new way. In the words of one Chicago priest who was close to the events, "There weren't these structures out there" that exist today to care for victims or report suspected abusers to law enforcement, and "The only other diocese at that time that was trying to stay ahead [of the problem] was Minneapolis-St. Paul."[17] Chicago was a pioneer in addressing the sexual abuse of minors years before the rest of the church came to grips with the problem, and Joseph was the leader. All over the United States and throughout the church, Joseph was recognized as "a leader in the Roman Catholic Church's recent efforts to detect and prevent sexual abuse by the clergy."[18]

Once the archdiocese's special commission recommended creating a body to investigate every allegation and report the allegations to law enforcement, Joseph implemented the plan immediately. More, he tried to share what he and the Archdiocese of Chicago had learned with his fellow bishops in the United States Conference of Catholic Bishops. He offered them Chicago's model that placed a layperson on the frontlines and reported every allegation. Always a proud member of the bishops' conference, Joseph wanted other bishops and the people in their dioceses to benefit from a hard lesson he had learned about a terrible problem. Yet Joseph's offer was rebuffed. One prominent cardinal-archbishop, whose own archdiocese later would experience a horrendous crisis over sexual abuse, is said to have dismissed Joseph's offer by saying that abusive priests were only "a Chicago problem." Several years later, after much more public embarrassment for church officials and much, much more suffering by victims, the bishops' conference did adopt national norms for dealing with sexual abuse. Those norms were very much like the Chicago model of 1992 and, sadly, even today not every diocese in the United States has adhered to them.

As we try to evaluate Joseph's role in the crisis of sexual abuse, we need to weigh the full sum of his actions and try to be honest about the bad and the good. The documentary record makes clear that it took Joseph some time to come to grips with the crisis, and during that time he did transfer abusive priests from one parish assignment to another with the hope that the abuse would not be repeated. Children were victimized as a result. But those facts need to be judged in context. Pedophilia has been recognized as a psychological disorder at least since the nineteenth century, but sustained psychological research into the phenomenon began just during the 1980s. Only quite recently has anyone come to understand how difficult pedophilia is to treat, or how stubbornly the disorder resists a cure. Our awareness that pedophilia can require ongoing treatment is quite new. It is a tragedy, and it does not absolve anyone, but Joseph and other Catholic bishops prior to the 1980s generally were acting on the best information available to anyone at the time. What we should say about Joseph is something a view of the man and his whole life would make obvious. He was capable of seeing the problem in a new light, getting past what he thought he knew about it, and taking decisive action to address the problem in light of new, better information once he had it. The 1991 scandal was a wake-up call to which he responded quickly and with determination. He was virtually alone among Catholic bishops for doing that. The structures that Joseph put into place in Chicago in 1992, in retrospect, offer a stinging indictment of nearly every other bishop in the United States who had the chance to learn from Joseph's experiences, had the chance to implement something like the Chicago model, and had the chance to prevent a lot of suffering. In the final analysis, Joseph possessed two characteristics that too many bishops did not possess. First, in the same way he was able to adapt to the reforms of the Second Vatican

Council and see the church anew, Joseph also was able to adapt to new information about sexual abuse. Second, while he was in Cincinnati, long before he arrived in Chicago, Joseph had adopted a focus on how his actions as archbishop affected "the people in the pews."[19] Or in the words of Chicago's Msgr. John Canary, "There was no one more sincere in wanting to address this than Cardinal Bernardin. . . . He was concerned about victims and he wanted to respond."[20]

There was another, less public dimension of Joseph's engagement with the problem of sexual abuse. The attention surrounding the crisis created a difficult climate even for priests who never had abused anyone. The archdiocese had taken a tough line with accused abusers. But false allegations sometimes were made, and innocent priests could be caught up in dreadful uncertainty while they awaited the conclusion of an embarrassing investigation. Priest morale suffered. Joseph, who had gone to such lengths when he arrived to reach out to and to become one of the priests of Chicago, could not have been unaware of this. He understood "very early on, that this was going to change even theologically his relationship with his priests," because "the necessary things that were being put in place were going to radically change the relationship of bishop and priest. It could no longer truly be a father-son relationship because he had legal responsibilities, and on this issue necessarily he had to be more attentive to parents and children."[21] A week after announcing the lay review board, Joseph offered a homily outside Chicago that touched on the nature of the priesthood:

> It is a lifelong challenge to surrender every dimension of our lives to God, holding nothing back from his loving care and the service of his people. Indeed, there are many

twists and turns in our lives. But in retrospect and in faith, we often see how God was present each moment, guiding and leading us. . . . In our priestly ministry, many of us have faced obstacles, opposition, and outright hostility. But the risen Lord has strengthened and sustained us in both good and difficult times. His Holy Spirit has guided and comforted us. At the same time, as his disciples, we have been called by Jesus to walk with him—on a journey that always leads to Jerusalem, a journey that always leads to suffering.[22]

We can hear Joseph's sense of the difficulties facing his Chicago priests in these remarks, difficulties to which he had recently become so alert.

These events were a continuation along a trajectory in Joseph's life that we might say began in Cincinnati, though really had begun before that. The same man who was described leaving Cincinnati as a pastor and who arrived at Chicago as a brother deepened his own spiritual life and his closeness to the people he served throughout his time in Chicago. In the teaching documents he published for the people of Chicago, we can see how a more intimate, caring, and spiritual focus begins to mark Joseph's approach. He had not abandoned his concern about war and peace or his devoted efforts to protect human life. Yet, the pastoral documents he produced after he had been in Chicago for a few years, such as The Family Gathered Here Before You (1989) or Here and Now (1994), reflect how he had shifted perspective. Documents about building the church community through a process of spiritual renewal and about engaging young people reflect the interests of a pastor who does not see the world flying fast from 35,000 feet above. Rather, they reflect the interest that Joseph had in each and every person in the Archdiocese of Chicago.

One example is Joseph's pastoral statement on the AIDS crisis, A Challenge and a Responsibility (1986). It may be difficult to remember looking back, but in those days homosexuality was not something so welcomed in American life as it is today. AIDS was a silent plague that hit the gay community hardest. Living, in a way, on the margins of American life, gay people faced the terrifying prospect of a deadly disease that too many leading Christians were quick to embrace as a punishment from God.[23] AIDS posed the Catholic Church with a difficult problem. Leaders like Joseph were torn between loyalty to church teaching that forbade homosexual acts and the ancient Christian duty to care for the sick and the weak. New York's Cardinal John O'Connor, with whom Joseph had worked so closely on The Challenge of Peace, exemplified the paradox facing church leaders. O'Connor attracted criticism for his outspoken condemnations of homosexuality and condom use. At the same time, he carried out a personal ministry to HIV-positive patients in a hospital designed for their care that he opened and blessed.

For the most part, Joseph avoided making stark or divisive public statements about the AIDS crisis. Joseph offered a measured statement on condom distribution that voiced his strong support for "informing the public, at all age levels, of the danger of AIDS" and at the same time said, "I am opposed to the general advertising of condoms because I cannot support advertising . . . which implicitly or explicitly condones promiscuity."[24] He kept the focus off condemning anyone and, much as O'Connor did, he began visiting AIDS patients at the two Catholic hospitals in the archdiocese that admitted and treated them. When he decided to issue a pastoral statement on the AIDS crisis, with his advisors he determined quickly to take an unusual approach. The statement begins with the story of Stephen, "a young man who died of AIDS. His story is not unique."[25] A Challenge and a Responsibility begins with that very personal story and builds up to a more broad teaching statement about how necessary it is for the church to be present to those who are suffering, especially to those who are sick. That corresponded to what anyone could see about Joseph's evolving pastoral style. But there was an even more human dimension at work as well in Joseph's AIDS ministry.

Stephen, who was described in A Challenge and a Responsibility, was based on a real person. It was not his real name, of course. Stephen had been in a relationship with a former priest whom Joseph had known in Cincinnati. Any bishop might have given into a temptation to shun a former priest who was gay. To be close to someone like that could feed scandal and rumors among those that want to sully a bishop who shows mercy and compassion to gay people. Like Jesus consorting with public sinners scandalized the Pharisees, there is a danger for a bishop who is seen with those who live on the margins. But when Stephen's partner had come to Chicago only six weeks after Stephen had died, Joseph stole time away from a banquet they were attending and consoled him. Father Michael Place remembered glimpsing Joseph and Stephen's partner sitting at a table amidst the crowd, just talking. They sat together for some time. No one else knows what was said. Afterwards, that former priest told Fr. Place that the experience had been "incredible." In their time sitting together amid a crowded dinner filled with people, he said, Joseph "was my pastor."[26] He had consoled him after the loss of someone he loved. For Joseph, and for the people of Chicago, encounters such as that one became the foundation for that compassionate, person-centered approach to AIDS ministry.

In all these ways, we see that the pastoral part of Joseph's personality had grown so much it now began to dominate his approach as archbishop. That development can be seen in big ways, like his growing reluctance to make decisions that would hurt large numbers of people even if the decisions were right. But we also can see it in small touches that brought joy or showed kindness even to one person like Stephen's partner. Monsignor Kenneth Velo recalled a particular incident around this time, one that reflects Joseph's style in a difficult pastoral situation as much as it brings a smile to the face. An elderly woman had written to Joseph after he announced the closure of Sacred Heart of Jesus Church, an old, ethnic Slovak parish in the Back of the Yards neighborhood. One morning, Joseph told Velo that he had written back and agreed to talk to the woman. They drove out to her home and the cardinal-archbishop of Chicago, a "prince of the church" and a global leader of moral and religious opinion, rang the doorbell of her bungalow at 71st and Hamlin. "That attention to people and individuals," Velo remembers, "the fact that he was there" in her living room and his desire to be present were what made him an effective pastor even in that difficult time.[27]

There are many similar stories that reveal how Joseph's emerging pastoral style made him such a fixture in and around Chicago. On one occasion, another one of Joseph's priest assistants remembered being out on Joseph's regular walk from the archbishop's residence in Lincoln Park down to the Chicago Water Tower and back up Lake Shore Drive. They came upon an elderly woman who was having difficulty crossing the street, and "the cardinal went up to her and didn't introduce himself, and he said, 'Are you going across the street?' And, she said, 'I am.' He said, 'I'll help you cross if you want to take my arm.' She said, 'Oh, that would be nice.' So they walk across the street, and they get to the other side. She looked at him and said, 'Well, thank you very much. I'm sure your wife wouldn't mind you doing this.'"[28] Another time, walking the same route one night after dark, they came across a group of men harassing two young women with vulgar talk. Joseph crossed the street, approached the women, "told them who he was, and he said, 'Father Donahue and I will now walk you home.'"[29] And they did.

All of these events express a truth that many people who knew Joseph attest to, but his assistant Ken Velo summarized best. "Everybody wanted to have a wonderfully close relationship with the cardinal, especially after he died," he recalls, "and, I'm a witness to this. . . . People would say things that he did that I know he did not do."[30] People recalled long conversations at dinners and events that, in fact, only lasted a moment. Some people told of encountering him walking through Lincoln Park, stopping and talking to them, even though Joseph's regular route did not take him through the park. This is the effect that affection has on memory. Like the fond biographies written about so many saints, an extraordinary person grows more extraordinary when remembered. And in those pastoral moments even before Joseph's extraordinary last days, despite all of the difficulties and struggles over parish closings or national politics, Joseph had won the love of the people of Chicago.

Even today, there is physical evidence of that love. Walk through Chicago's near north side and enter Holy Name Cathedral through the main entrance on State Street. Find yourself in the narthex and look to your right. A bronze plaque on the wall lists the names of Chicago's archbishops. Even from where you stand, just inside the door, you'll see from a distance that one name appears faded, less distinct than the others. Walk closer and see that it is Joseph Cardinal Bernardin. His name is worn from the fingers of so many people who have touched it.

CHAPTER FIVE

A Challenge and Peace
(1993–96)

The Catholic Church was changing as the 1990s began. It was happening in the United States and all around the world. In large part the change was due to the length of the John Paul II papacy. John Paul II and the prefect for the Congregation of the Doctrine of the Faith, Cardinal Joseph Ratzinger, both had been present at the Second Vatican Council. Both had been known throughout the church and the theological community as council liberals. But the decades of experimentation that followed the council created a backlash. The 1980s was a period during which church officials began talking about reining in some of the council's excesses, which may have been fair enough in some cases. More often than not, the pope and Cardinal Ratzinger were the ones pressing the brake pedal on post-council experimentation and reform. Both men still were devoted to the council, but had become concerned about a spirit of reform they felt threatened to overtake the council's theological foundations. This drift of events slowly began to forge a rough alliance between John Paul II and conservative voices in the church who never had been enthusiastic about the council. As just one example, Pope John Paul granted permission in 1984 for limited use of the Latin Mass, and Pope Benedict removed even that limitation in 2007. The change delighted longtime opponents of liturgical reform and cemented deep divisions over liturgy into a permanent, defining split in practice. John Paul's long papacy provided stability within which skeptics about the council's reform could refight battles lost in the 1960s and 1970s and, as 1990 drew near, that change of direction was becoming difficult not to notice.

Joseph had begun the 1980s as the most prominent Catholic bishop in the United States—arguably, he was even more prominent than that. When John Paul appointed Joseph to Chicago, he told him, "I know that the way the church in the United States goes is the way the church in the world will go. And, I know that the way that the church in Chicago goes is the way the church in the United States will go. So, I'm putting all my trust in you."[1] Pope John Paul had personally seen that Joseph was appointed to Chicago, and he elevated Joseph to the cardinalate less than a year later. Of course, Joseph's personal imprint was fixed on the bishops' conference, and it was impossible for him not to have great influence at meetings. Several times through the 1980s, Joseph was dispatched quietly to address problems in other dioceses as an honest broker trusted both by Rome and by American bishops. Beyond any doubt, Joseph Bernardin was the most influential churchman in the Western world.

As the 1980s faded into the 1990s, Rome's esteem for Joseph seemed suddenly to ebb. Some of the officials in the Vatican offices had begun to fear Joseph's influence had grown too great, and several appointments of new bishops

in the United States were much different sorts of person-
alities, more eager to confront secular culture than to reach
out to it. Those appointments could be seen as a conscious
effort to offset Joseph's influence and the influence of other
bishops who were like him. Joseph began to sense a growing
isolation, and sometimes his fall from influence was less
than subtle. In 1987 Joseph traveled to Rome for a meeting
of bishops from around the world. Such meetings were
lengthy and large. One day after a break for lunch, Joseph
was the among first to return to the meeting hall where he
found that photocopies of a newspaper article attacking him
had been left on each bishop's seat. Joseph saw some of the
bishops smiling and snickering when they observed his
shocked reaction. This was an extraordinary breach not just
of protocol, but also security. Unless some stranger had
found a way into the room to leave the copies, they must
have been left on the chairs by some bishop or cardinal from
the Holy See. These were schoolyard tactics, but they signaled to Joseph how it had become acceptable among some
number of powerful churchmen to reject his leadership.
Surely, in part, this also was a consequence of Joseph's iden-
tification of a consistent ethic that stretches across all the
life issues from abortion to war and peace. He had waded
in controversy, and now came the blowback.

   This information provides the necessary context for how
a false allegation of sexual misconduct against Joseph came
to change his life forever. It was November 1993 when Joseph
first heard a rumor that a cardinal would be accused of sexual abuse. He was staying with Cardinal John O'Connor in
New York, where he gave a speech at Columbia University.
Upon his return to Chicago the next day, the speculation had
coalesced around Joseph. This was simply stunning, particularly given the way that the accusation had wafted across the

United States first as a vague rumor. The details of the accusation, which had not been reported to law enforcement, first came to light in a television interview and then in a lawsuit. It all seemed like a calculated attack. It shocked Joseph to be charged with an allegation he knew was false. Where once he had been, beyond question, the most respected and influential Catholic churchman in the United States, one of the most in the world, by 1993 there were forces at work in the church eager to take him down.

Every appearance tells us that it was Joseph's sensitive outreach to victims of AIDS and gay people that may have provoked this attack. Joseph wrote in *The Gift of Peace*, and other reporting subsequent to his death seems to confirm, that the allegation began at the instigation of a Wisconsin priest who, even years after Joseph died, regularly wrote against homosexual conspiracies in the church. That priest had been a harsh critic of Joseph for all sorts of things, at one point calling Joseph "an evil man."[2] That Wisconsin priest had come to know a troubled young man named Steven Cook through a New Jersey attorney who specialized in clergy sex abuse cases. After treatment by a hypnotist at the encouragement of the priest and the attorney, Steven thought he recovered a memory of having been abused by Joseph.

In truth, Fr. Michael Place got it just right when he said that it would be "unfortunate" for all of these lurid details to distract us too much.[3] By itself, the whole event amounted to nothing much more than a troubled young man who was manipulated by others against his will to humiliate Joseph. The allegation became public in a carefully orchestrated television interview that was timed to the filing of a civil suit, which speaks eloquently to the sordidness of the whole episode. It does not reflect much on Joseph's life. The accusation was so flimsy, perhaps from our perspective today, it seems inevitable that the scandal collapsed in only a few months when Steven Cook recanted and asked a federal judge to dismiss the suit. But what those details tell us are how determined some people were to "get" Joseph. They alert us to a kind of rancor that had set into the church. They also make clear the type and the depth of the suffering that those people chose to inflict on Joseph, to discredit his vision for the church.[4]

Over and over, people describe Joseph as a reconciler. He had a personality that sought to bring people together, overcome differences, and minimize conflict. It is difficult to imagine a darker purgatory for a reconciler than to face people so implacable they will not relent in conflict—especially when the allegation was so personal and humiliating as the one leveled against Joseph, because it questioned his most fundamental commitment as a pastor, the care of persons. For all these reasons, the months from November 1993 until March 1994 were a crucible that tested Joseph's faith. Many holy people have experienced something similar to this. Saint Thérèse of Lisieux and Saint John of the Cross have left us a treasure of spiritual writings in which they describe their own testing in darkness. Mother Theresa of Calcutta felt abandoned by God at times throughout her life. We do not know whether Joseph looked to any of those spiritual models for comfort or how much comfort he may have drawn from them during those difficult weeks, but his own marvelous spiritual testimonial emerged from the event:

> To close the gap between what I am and what God wants of me, I must empty myself and let Jesus come in and take over. I have prayed to understand his agenda for me. Some things stand out. He wants me to focus on the *essentials* of his message and way of life rather than on the accidentals that needlessly occupy so much of our time and efforts.

> One can easily distinguish essentials from peripherals in the spiritual life. Essentials ask us to give true witness and to love others more. Nonessentials close us in on ourselves. It is unsettling to pray to be emptied of self; it seems a challenge almost beyond our reach as humans. But if we try, I have learned, God does most of the work.[5]

In the depths of this experience of emptying, Joseph found the resources to become even more fully who he was.

The Steven Cook episode deserves our attention because of what it showed us about Joseph, and because of what it allowed him to understand better about himself. The effect appears to have come over him rather quickly. In an intense meeting as the scandal broke, Joseph rejected the "scorched earth" strategy recommended by attorneys and preferred, instead, to hold a press conference simply to proclaim the truth of his innocence. There would be no countersuits or other aggressive tactics used against Joseph's accuser. Joseph even would report himself to the commission he created a year earlier to investigate abuse claims. Only a week after the accusation, he told a gathering of Chicago priests that he understood what happened as "a moment of grace" and an opportunity for "spiritual growth."[6] Yet, while Joseph was quick to recognize that he was experiencing something extraordinary and important, we should not suppose it was easy for him.

Father Scott Donahue compared the time to Christ's agony in the garden, a lonely and direct encounter with God through suffering that brought out of Joseph some measure of peace in the face of what had been set before him. "He trusted his own good relationship with the Lord" to see him through the trial.[7] Monsignor Ken Velo called the Steven Cook experience "a conversion event" that he likened to Joseph's recommitment to prayer while he was archbishop of Cincinnati.[8] Yet "he suffered terribly," and, in the end, Donahue suggests that the accusation, perhaps literally, "worried him to death."[9] Joseph's father had died early from cancer, and certainly that meant that Joseph was at some increased risk to face the disease. Whether or not the illness that would take Joseph's life had some relationship to the suffering he endured during the accusation is not something anyone can say. But those closest to Joseph believe that it did. They believe that the toll on Joseph, his worry about the effect on the public ministry he had built for decades and his own personal integrity, brought on the cancer that manifested itself barely a year after Steven Cook recanted.

Joseph's suffering did end, at least for a time, after the accusation was withdrawn. The year between the accusation and Joseph's cancer diagnosis brought a burst of energy from him. A new light shone from him. He threw himself into his work with a renewed vigor, perhaps with a feeling of liberation that he had faced the trial, he had held to the truth, he had been vindicated, and through all that he had deepened his spiritual relationship with God. In a way, he even enjoyed a more particular sort of encouragement after Steven Cook recanted when Joseph received a phone call from Pope John Paul. In those days, popes did not simply pick up the telephone, and Joseph first thought his aides were pulling his leg when told: "The pope is on the phone." Joseph took the call, and Pope John Paul poured out his relief and his joy that Joseph had been so fully vindicated. After all that had happened during the last several years when he had seen so many people resist his efforts to bring the church together over the council's vision, Joseph got a shot in the arm that made him bold, gave him the confidence to press forward with his ministry into new directions.

This was the time during which Joseph made his historic trip to the Holy Land, an event that affirmed the close bond between him and the Jewish community that he had worked for so many years to cultivate and nurture. Until 1993, because the Holy See had not recognized the Israeli state diplomatically, senior churchmen generally did not visit Israel. Joseph was the first cardinal to lead an interfaith journey to the Holy Land. The delegation consisted of rabbis, Catholic clergy, and women religious. Their eight days brought them to the holy sites of Judaism, Christianity, and Islam, as well as to the memorial and world center for Holocaust research, Yad Vashem. Joseph met with Israeli and Palestinian political leaders, as well as leaders of the Roman Catholic and Greek Orthodox churches in the Holy Land. At Hebrew University of Jerusalem, Joseph was invited to lecture; he chose as his topic the responsibility of Christians for anti-Semitism. Restating the Second Vatican Council's embrace of the Jewish community and Pope John Paul's condemnation of anti-Semitism as a sin, Joseph went farther to say, "much more needs to be done."[10] Pointing to resurgences of anti-Semitism around the globe, Joseph called for concrete, even difficult, steps to be taken. "The history of anti-Semitism and of anti-Judaic theology," he said, "must be restored to our Catholic teaching materials."[11] Joseph said, "The Catholic Church must be prepared to submit its World War II record to a thorough scrutiny by respected scholars."[12] He added that the liturgical seasons must "become times of reconciliation between Jews and Christians rather than conflict and division."[13] These were frank, honest assessments that demanded looking directly at unpleasant truths, resolving to move forward past the reach of a dreadful history. After Joseph died, Jewish leaders came to Holy Name Cathedral to pray over his body. The *Chicago Tribune* described the incongruity of the scene, "rabbis offering eulogies before a massive golden crucifix," and yet observed that the strangeness was overwhelmed by how well suited the gesture was "to the moment and the man they honored." The *Tribune* quoted Rabbi Herman Schaalman, a pillar of the Jewish community in Chicago, saying, "Never in the history of this world has such an event taken place." It was Joseph, with all he had done and said, who had made the moment seem natural.[14]

The bold voice that Joseph found to push so energetically on important issues like Catholic-Jewish dialogue was only one sign of the depth of the conversion experience Joseph had because of the abuse allegation. Yet one last thing was necessary truly to move forward into this new part of his life. Joseph felt strongly he had to meet with Steven Cook. He could not move past the event without, at least, an attempt to reconcile with his accuser and make peace with him. Joseph reached out to Steven's mother through a priest in Cincinnati, and she replied that her son wanted to see Joseph. A meeting was set.

Joseph flew to Philadelphia on December 30, 1994, to meet with Steven Cook and his partner, Kevin. Father Scott Donahue traveled with Joseph to Philadelphia, and he remembers that the meeting happened "exactly" the same way that Joseph described it in *The Gift of Peace*. What happened, as Joseph described it, simply was extraordinary. It was a "profound reconciliation."[15] The four men sat quietly together. They talked. Steven described how he had been manipulated to include Joseph in his lawsuit. They reconciled. Hesitantly, Joseph offered Steven a gift—a Bible. Steven, who once had been a seminarian, but who had grown so angry at God and at the church, accepted the gift, and Joseph said Mass for the four of them. After Mass, Joseph administered the sacrament of anointing of the sick to Steven, who was suffering from AIDS. Afterwards Joseph recalled that he had said, "In every family there are times when there is hurt, anger, or alienation. But we cannot run away from our family. We have only one family and so, after every falling out, we must make every effort to be reconciled. So, too, the church is our spiritual family. Once we become a member, we may be hurt or become alienated, but it is still our family. Since there is no other, we must work at reconciliation. And that is what we have been doing this very afternoon."[16] The six-year-old boy who had seen his father die too soon, who saw his mother widowed with two small children and felt his extended family close around him in those difficult days had nurtured that idea. The young man who had come to understand that the priesthood was an even better way to help people than studying medicine had placed his hopes in that idea. The priest-administrator who worked so tirelessly making certain that the practical needs of the church and its people were met felt a responsibility rooted in that idea. The youngest bishop in America embraced this idea in the Second Vatican Council and its vision of the whole people of God gathered together as a family. He labored to make the American bishops a model of that family through the building up of the bishops' conference. In Cincinnati, he rediscovered his own place in that family when he deepened his relationship with God through prayer. And now, Joseph who had been tested so terribly by the trial of a false accusation came back to that idea in order to give a gift of reconciliation and peace to his accuser. Steven died not quite ten months later. He died in his mother's home at peace with himself, with Joseph, and with God. Before he died, he was received back into the Catholic Church. By the grace of God, the false accusation had provided the opportunity for the shepherd to recover the lost sheep. Suffering became a grace for both men and, through their determination to share the experience, for others as well.

Joseph spoke of a lightness he felt in those days, and how could he not? But just as all those experiences before the Steven Cook accusation were a preparation for the reconciliation Joseph would make with him, the extraordinary grace he received through the experience of being falsely accused only prepared him for one more trial. Ken Velo recalls that Joseph used to say, "The three things I really was concerned about were that I would get cancer, that there would be a false allegation against me, and that I would die from cancer."[17] How could those things not have concerned Joseph? Cancer had scarred his young life, and Joseph had seen the power of an accusation of sexual misconduct, whether true or false, in his work as a bishop. Yet, in due course, those three worst fears would come to him as realities. And he would be prepared.

The first sign that something may have been wrong appeared one night in June 1995. Within days, physicians at Mercy Hospital confirmed a cancer diagnosis. Joseph had a malignant tumor on his pancreas. Surgery was scheduled for a few days later, barely a week after the first symptoms appeared. Joseph recalled getting the news from his doctors. When they gave him the news, the shock was overwhelming—so was a feeling of something resembling betrayal. After everything that had happened to him in the previous year during the trying experience of the false allegation, Joseph had regained a sense of control over his life. Throughout his life Joseph, a careful administrator, always had delighted in a feeling of control. His hard work and attention to detail made possible so many successes in Charleston, Atlanta, Washington, Cincinnati, and Chicago. The loss of control Joseph felt after the accusation may have been the most difficult part of the experience for him, even as it also was the most important. With the Steven Cook accusation,

Joseph had learned how important it is to let go and to trust God. Now with a cancer diagnosis, he recalled that lesson quickly. He embraced whatever lay ahead. With suddenness, though surely not without difficulty, Joseph came to the realization of his life's end—both its termination and its purpose. He determined quickly to share that realization. He called a press conference for June 9, where his doctors explained to Chicago and the world what had happened to Joseph, and what *would* happen to him. Joseph chose quite deliberately to be public about his illness. He told Ken Velo, "I have to show the people what I've been teaching them all these years."[18]

In *The Gift of Peace*, Joseph credits the spiritual writer Henri Nouwen with helping him find peace with this new suffering and the prospect of his own death. Joseph had known Nouwen since his time in Washington with the bishops' conference, and not long after the cancer diagnosis Nouwen paid a visit to Chicago. By coincidence, Nouwen just had published a book about death and dying. The timing was fortunate for Joseph. In their meeting Nouwen said to him, "People of faith, who believe that death is the transition from this life to eternal life, should see it as a friend."[19] Joseph would come to embrace death as his friend, not as a terrible prospect to be dreaded and feared. Certainly the prospect of illness and death still frightened him. Even the deepest faith must face from time to time the reality that faith is belief. Faith does not offer factual certainty. To approach death as a friend does not switch off those natural human reactions, and Nouwen does not encourage us at all to think that way: "It somehow doesn't take death seriously enough to say to a dying person, 'Don't be afraid. After your death you will be resurrected as Jesus was, meet all your friends again, and be happy forever in the presence of God.' This suggests that after death everything will be basically the same, except that our troubles will be gone."[20] Death is a more profound event. It must fill us with greater awe than walking into a surprise party, and with that awe comes uncertainty.

To see death as a friend means to see death as a part of a Christian life. Death is life's inevitable end. Yet, Christian life is life with Christ. So, Christian death is death with him. For the believer, death is the summit toward which a Christian life has aimed. It is the moment that calls us to recognize, even if we have lived a Christian life, whether we are prepared to accept fully that step beyond certainty and into the fullness of what faith demands from us. We must make the leap. If we have lived a life of faith, we can come to the suffering of dying and death as the challenge we have accepted throughout our life. We embrace it as what our life has meant. This was Joseph's message to the people of Chicago and the world through his illness and suffering.

The surgery went well. The surgeons removed one of Joseph's kidneys, which the cancer had invaded, as well as the top half of his pancreas that contained the tumor. Tissue from other organs was removed, as well as several lymph nodes in order to try to gather any cancerous tissue that may have spread. After the surgery a program of chemotherapy and radiation continued his treatment. As he recovered from the surgery and continued his treatment through the summer of 1995, Joseph began what he called his cancer ministry. Even while recuperating from surgery, Joseph visited with other patients on his floor at Loyola University Medical Center. He and the other cancer patients he met through his treatment kept up a close relationship over the next several months.

Joseph kept up his commitments as archbishop during this time and worked as much as his energy would permit.

Yet nothing restored his energy more than contact with the people he met through his cancer ministry. Ken Velo remembered how he would call one of them on the phone if Joseph was tired or had a difficult day, and he would pass the phone to Joseph: "I would call some of those people, and I'd say, 'Lottie, how are you? Just checking in.' And then I'd push the hold button on her call, and I'd call on the intercom and say, 'Cardinal, Lottie's on the phone.' And he may have thought that Lottie called him. But he was able to talk to her. I was able to see her phone line lighted up for a good deal of time while they talked about what was going on."[21] Certainly, this is an experience that many people facing a difficult diagnosis have had. There is a unique way that people experiencing the same suffering can comfort and strengthen one another. Joseph drew strength from those contacts, no doubt. He received cards, letters, and all kinds of messages from other cancer patients he never would be able to meet face to face, but he reached out with phone calls or cards to as many as he could. For Joseph this new ministry had another, deeper dimension. Through his illness and suffering, Joseph found an even more profound calling as a pastor.

Joseph's ministry continued in other ways, too. The Catholic Common Ground Initiative came about because of a pastoral statement Joseph issued in 1992, The Parish in the Contemporary Church. Joseph had grown concerned that controversies in the church that followed the council were beginning to affect parish life. The pastoral statement expressed that concern, and it prompted a phone call to Joseph from Msgr. Philip Murnion, a researcher at the National Pastoral Life Center (NPLC). Murnion was a sociologist and the director of the NPLC, which the bishops' conference had created in 1983 to study and support the church's pastoral ministry, especially at the parish level. Murnion shared Joseph's concern. The pastoral statement had made Murnion wonder whether Joseph might like to join him and lead an effort to build bridges not only within parishes, but within the church more generally. Very quietly, he and Joseph invited many prominent Catholics from all over the United States and from every perspective to begin a dialogue about finding common ground within the church. Over time, in consultation with many others, a statement was drafted—Called to Be Catholic: Church in a Time of Peril.

Joseph's remarks at an August 12, 1996, press conference announcing the Catholic Common Ground Initiative deserve special attention. He knew by then that his life was near its end, and he had been through the crucible experiences of the false allegation and the cancer diagnosis. This was a time to sum up his life and his ministry, to say what was important and bequeath to the church a lasting legacy. Early in his remarks he cited the influence on his life and priesthood of Paul Hallinan and John Dearden, from whom he had learned "to trust that, through open and honest dialogue, differences can be resolved and the integrity of the gospel proclaimed."[22] The call to dialogue does not abandon the truth of faith, and it poses us with nothing that should frighten us. He went on to trace the commitment to dialogue throughout his ministry, and then noted that, "I have been troubled that an increasing polarization within the Church and, at times, a mean-spiritedness have hindered the kind of dialogue that helps us address our mission and concerns. As a result, the unity of the Church is threatened, the great gift of the Second Vatican Council is in danger of being seriously undermined, the faithful members of the Church are weary, and our witness to government, society, and culture is compromised."[23] We sense the weight of how Joseph himself experienced that polarization during the decade preceding the news conference, and we also see how much Joseph felt his whole life had prepared him to address the problem.

Joseph was not prepared for the reaction. Some of Joseph's most senior confreres, American cardinal-archbishops, issued public statements critical of the Common Ground Initiative that seemed almost to question Joseph's motives. Philadelphia's Cardinal Anthony Bevilacqua said, "A polite debate or a respectful exchange of divergent views about what would be the most commonly acceptable Catholic teaching is not sufficient to adequately address and heal the differences which exist among the faithful." Detroit's Cardinal Adam Maida wrote, "We do not 'dialogue' about membership in the church." And Boston's Cardinal Bernard Law concluded that, "Dialogue as a way to mediate between truth and dissent is mutual deception." This was not only a wholesale rejection of an approach to the problem that had been constructed carefully over years and among many people. But worse, this was a public breach. Observers noted how "unusual" this public disagreement was among senior churchmen who could not seem to find common ground for a discussion of common ground.[24]

But this public disagreement also was peculiar. Joseph had spent his whole ministry doing precisely what he did in Common Ground. He worked with all of the parties, brought everyone together, and searched for the way forward that could bring everyone along. He had built up the bishops' conference on just that same model of working together. He never blindsided anyone. In fact, Joseph had circulated Called to Be Catholic before its public release, and he had phoned those other cardinals personally before the news conference. There was no whiff of an objection to anything Joseph proposed before he announced it publicly.

The objections only came later, and Joseph was stung by it. It was for that reason that several of those closest to him remembered that the public criticism surrounding Common Ground hurt Joseph even more than the false accusation had hurt him.

It was against that difficult backdrop that the final chapter of Joseph's life unfolded. Having worked for years to build up the unity of the church in the spirit of the Second Vatican Council, and having himself been at the center of most of the political controversies that swirled around the church during the last half of the twentieth century, Joseph ended his life with a thoughtful plea for unity, dialogue, and common ground. He left that work unfinished, though not for lack of any effort.

As the second half of 1996 began, Joseph's health problems seemed both to have worsened and improved. The radiation treatments had taken a toll on his bones, weakening them so that they fractured easily. This was painful and, to some degree, dangerous. Joseph fell a few times, once while he was alone in his home. Unable to get up, he had to crawl to a telephone to get help. In all, he fractured four vertebrae and four ribs during that time. Probably worst was the weakness in his legs that caused the falling, and it was accompanied by pain in his back whenever he walked, stood, or sat. Eventually the doctors diagnosed spinal stenosis, a painful narrowing of the spinal canal that compresses the nerves.

On the other hand, after his primary course of radiation and chemotherapy had ended, Joseph began what doctors called a maintenance program. A weekly injection hoped to maintain a defense against the recurrence of cancer, and as late as August 27 the regular screenings and tests he underwent showed no sign that the disease had returned. With an otherwise clean bill of health, his physicians planned spinal surgery that would relieve the pain and weakness caused by the stenosis. Everything looked great.

But a routine MRI ahead of the surgery, one last look to be sure Joseph was cancer free, revealed the cancer had returned. Several tumors had appeared on his liver, one of them rather large, and the prognosis was grim. His physician, Dr. Ellen Gaynor, OP, told him he had perhaps a year to live. This changed everything.

Ken Velo remembers the drive home from that meeting with Dr. Gaynor: "I was worried about that ride back. On the ride back, he made calls to his sister, he made calls to— he called my parents to tell them. He said, 'I don't want you to hear this on the news.' That's what hit me. My parents. He knew them; he spent a Christmas with us. But, you know, he had so many other people he could have called."[25] Joseph already had befriended death. He was unprepared for the bad news. He was surprised. Certainly, he was afraid. Yet he found quickly that he was at peace. We can see that peace in how little he dwelled in those worst first moments on himself, and how thoughtful he was even to think of Velo and his parents.

Joseph came back to the microphones in an August 30 news conference to tell the world about his diagnosis. Of course the spinal surgery was canceled. The focus now was on the end of his life. There were preparations to make for the archdiocese, and there were his affairs to get in order. At the end of September, Joseph made a final journey to Italy. The purpose of his journey was to meet with Pope John Paul and to report on his health. Surely, their conversation also touched on the future of the archdiocese, their shared experience of suffering, and the bond of friendship they had forged since Joseph first visited Poland many years before. But the most important part of the journey for Joseph may have been his final visit to Assisi, which came after meeting with the Holy Father. There, with his fellow Franciscans, he offered a Mass for his other religious community, the priests of the Archdiocese of Chicago. This was a happy and relaxing time, before the disease began to rob him of the energy to perform even basic tasks. That would come quickly after his return to Chicago.

Joseph's spiritual connection to Saint Francis seems to have been very much in his mind during his last days. He told Fr. Al Spilly that he wanted to die without any possessions. He wanted to leave the world poor, just as he had entered it, in just the way that St. Francis had given up his possessions. Giving things away kept Joseph busy, but it seemed also to fill him with joy. Even today, his friends treasure the things he so thoughtfully gave them. Joseph gave his watch to Fr. Scott Donahue, engraved with a message of friendship. Father Michael Place remembers the note that accompanied Joseph's briefcase when Ken Velo brought it to him: "This briefcase carried only the most important documents, many of which came from you. How fitting it is that you should have it."[26] To Spilly, Joseph left the crucifix that hung over his own bed for twenty-five years, which he had described in *The Gift of Peace*. Each gift was thoughtfully set aside for each person. Ken Velo also remembered another detail that Joseph did not overlook. Joseph telephoned him one day in July:

> He said, "I'd love to go to the Merchandise Mart and get Christmas gifts." . . . I picked him up. We went to the Merchandise Mart, went to a few places . . . and he bought about twenty-five things. They were all to be delivered to the residence. When August came, they were up in the attic. The terminal diagnosis came just a number of weeks after

that. . . . The day of the funeral, I went to his desk to write some notes [for the homily]. Now, I was the executor of his estate, and so I looked through the drawers of his desk. . . . I opened the file drawer, where he kept the files. On top of the files, perpendicular, was this manila folder. It said, "Ken, here's the Christmas list. Thank you."[27]

Joseph had considered every detail, made every thoughtful gesture to every person he could. But one bitterly painful task remained. Joseph would have to make sure that his mother was cared for. Maria Simion Bernardin would out-live her Joe.

By this time, Maria was nearing ninety-two years old. For many years, she had lived in a facility overseen by the Little Sisters of the Poor just a short drive away from the arch-bishop's residence. Joseph had moved her there not very long after he came to Chicago, and if he was not traveling he paid her at least a short visit every day. Maria was in the twilight of senescence by this time. She was still very much herself, so far as her personality was intact. She reacted to questions and to people much as she always did. She did not always recognize people though; her memory had failed her. It is not certain that she always recognized Joseph. Yet her visits with Joseph, and with Ken Velo who often ac-companied him, must always have brightened her day. Jo-seph certainly felt the burden of leaving her behind. Maria had carried such a heavy load after Giuseppe died, returning to work so she could support her two children. Joseph had been a good son. He had cared for his mother and arranged that she would be cared for until she died. But now he would leave her, and that was the hardest part of this last chapter for him. Ken Velo remembers asking Joseph about two weeks before he died if he wanted to visit his mother. Joseph said he was tired, and certainly he was. Velo sensed something else, too. It was near the end, and "he did not want to go back to his mother's because he did not want to say goodbye."[28] It simply was too painful.

The end now was coming with shocking quickness. As October ended, Joseph gave up the day-to-day management of the archdiocese. He rested and focused on preparing *The Gift of Peace* as a final testament to his life and ministry. The book is a powerful message about dying and living, a testimony to how Joseph's spiritual life had grown and matured over time to help him embrace death as his friend. Just days before he died, with his distinctive penmanship, Joseph wrote the titles for the book's chapters and hand wrote an introduction that can be found in the book's first edition. It is an extraordinary farewell that also stands as an invitation to Christian life for anyone who reads it.

Joseph died early in the morning of November 14, 1996. It was Maria's birthday, and just three days before the 95th anniversary of Giuseppe's arrival in the United States. Their son Joe died a bishop and cardinal, a respected leader of the church, and an admired voice for peace and reconciliation. He had received the Medal of Freedom, the highest award the President of the United States can give to a civilian. He had met presidents and joined in political debates to try to build a more just and peaceful world. In pursuit of those high goals, he succeeded better than many people have. Dignitaries of all sorts filed into his funeral Mass at Holy Name Cathedral, while ordinary people stood outside, lined the streets for his funeral procession, and stopped what they were doing to watch the Mass on television. They all responded to Joseph with love because that was what he had given to them. More than that, he had shown them how to love one another. He had been their pastor.

Conclusion

Joseph Bernardin's death and funeral brought Chicago to a halt.

Catholics and non-Catholics kept vigil and mourned him. Television programs were interrupted. People broke away from work midday on a Wednesday to watch the Mass. Thousands lined the streets to offer a final farewell. Even in a city so deeply Catholic as Chicago, it is difficult to imagine something else that could command the attention of so many diverse people in every, unavoidable way. More than that, the world mourned on November 20, 1996. Maybe the death of a president or a pope might be comparable, but Joseph was neither. His accomplishment and stature were different. Joseph had moved people in a personal and lasting way.

Joseph led an extraordinary life. Yet it was the manner of his dying and death that captured people's imaginations. To say he was courageous in the face of illness somehow misses the mark. To accept death as a friend, and to talk about that with such certain reassurance, was something other than courage. It was faith.

Joseph had some advantages in his faith-filled approach to living and dying. He had watched his mother courageously and selflessly support her family. He had been nurtured by the extended family that helped them. He had seen two father figures suffer and die. He was too young to be of any help to his father, Giuseppe, but that death loomed over the rest of his life. When the time came to minister to his friend and mentor, Paul Hallinan, Joseph already knew life in the context of suffering and death. With Hallinan, he had the chance to reflect even further on the meaning of suffering and what it means to live a Christian life that must, inevitably, end in death. We know that Joseph was able to comfort Hallinan during his illness, and we can presume that Hallinan remained a model for Joseph's life and ministry, his living and his dying.

Hallinan provided another sort of model as well. So did John Dearden. Both men were older than Joseph, yet both were priests from a generation before the Second Vatican Council, just like him. Joseph saw both Hallinan and Dearden change with the times and embrace a new way to think about the church. For Joseph, who was ordained thirteen years before the council ended, that could have been a difficult thing to do. Yet for him, it was easier because he had watched both Hallinan and Dearden and learned from them. In another sense, it was perhaps easier for Joseph than it was for Hallinan, Dearden, or many other priests of his time. Joseph was the child of immigrants. From a very young age, he would have felt connected to the old world that his family left for America. Throughout his life, Joseph's Italian heritage remained important, and he maintained relationships with family members in Tonadico. Like all children of immigrants, Joseph also was his family's connection to the new world. In this way, he learned throughout his life how to manage transition. No better skill could have served him during his life and ministry and, if we think about it, perhaps there is no more distinctively American trait than to feel this way. So many Americans descend from immigrants, carry the immigrant experience in their hearts and minds, that to feel rooted in the old world while reaching into the promise of the new world is a special contribution that Americans like Hallinan, Dearden, and Joseph have given to the church. That same rootedness in one place while straining to reach the next place also is a very fine metaphor for Christian life. We live in this world. We long for the next.

In these ways, Joseph Bernardin's life that began in the long shadow of the Dolomite peaks of northern Italy and brought him to rest in a crypt built over the dolomite bedrock that lies beneath the Chicago region, seems as though it could have been no other way. That is not true, of course, and Joseph would not have accepted such a pat explanation. We all are given these opportunities in our lives. Grace comes to everyone. To seize the opportunity that is grace, "to be fully and authentically human, therefore, means striving for the highest sanctity" in all that we do.[1] That work is ours to do with what we each are given.

True to his namesake, Joseph the Worker, that was Joseph Bernardin's message for us all. "We have work to do—our share in restoring all things in Christ. We must take off the blinders, so that we can see 'the splendor of the gospel showing forth the glory of Christ, the image of God' "(2 Cor 4:4).[2]

Notes

Chapter One:
An Immigrant Family (1928–66)—pages 3–23

1. Like many immigrant names, the spelling of Joseph's father's name is inconsistent in the documentary record. For simplicity, I have chosen to call him Giuseppe.

2. Anita Bernardin Orf interview with author, October 28, 2014, Columbia, SC.

3. Joseph L. Bernardin, *The Gift of Peace* (Chicago: Loyola Press, 1997), 63.

4. Thomas McLean, "Cardinal Bernardin," *The State* (January 30, 1983), 5B.

5. Cathleen Falsani, "Beloved Cousin Joe Is Missed Already," *Chicago Tribune* (November 18, 1996).

6. McLean, "Cardinal Bernardin," 5B.

7. Ibid.

8. Ibid.

9. Hanke Gratteau, "Bernardin Clan's Trip Here a Thrill," *Chicago Sun-Times* (August 25, 1982), 1.

10. McLean, "Cardinal Bernardin," 5B.

11. Eugene Kennedy, *My Brother Joseph: The Spirit of a Cardinal and the Story of a Friendship* (New York: St. Martin's Press, 1997), 2.

12. Kenneth Velo interview with author, March 18, 2015, Chicago, IL.

13. Eugene Kennedy, *Bernardin: Life to the Full* (Chicago: Bonus Books, 1997), 23.

14. McLean, "Cardinal Bernardin," 5B.

15. Ibid.

16. Ibid.,1.

17. Joseph L. Bernardin to Most Reverend E.M. Walsh (June 6, 1945), Personnel—Bernardin, Joseph L., 1945–1982, Priest Subject Files, Diocese of Charleston Archives, Charleston, SC.

18. John L. Manning to Very Reverend Lloyd P. McDonald, SS, (February 19, 1948), *PSF*, Folder: Personnel—Bernardin, Joseph L., 1945–1982.

19. Untitled remarks on being named auxiliary bishop of Atlanta (undated), Joseph Louis Bernardin Collection, Speeches & Talks, Folder, Talks—1965 & Prior, Archives of the Archdiocese of Chicago, Chicago, IL.

20. Bishop John J. Russell to Rev. Alfred F. Kamler (December 14, 1951), *PSF*, Folder: Personnel—Bernardin, Joseph L., 1945–1982.

21. Thomas J. Shelley, *Paul J. Hallinan: First Archbishop of Atlanta* (Wilmington, DE: Michael Glazier, Inc., 1989), 85. Shelley cites the description with an interview he conducted with Cardinal Bernardin in Chicago on October 3, 1985.

22. Joseph L. Bernardin, "Diocese of Charleston: 1958–1962" (undated), *PSF*, Folder: Bernardin, Joseph L., 1962–2002 and undated, 1.

23. Kennedy, *Bernardin: Life to the Full*, 28.

24. Shelley, *Paul J. Hallinan*, 91.

25. Quoted at Shelley, 104.

26. "The Church and the Negro" (no date), *JLB*, Speeches & Talks, Folder "Talks—1965 and Prior," 8.

27. R. Bentley Anderson, *Black, White, and Catholic: New Orleans Interracialism, 1947–1956* (Nashville: Vanderbilt University Press, 2005), 61.

28. "To: KofC" (1965), *JLB*, Speeches & Talks, Folder "Talks—1965 and Prior," 5.

29. Paul J. Hallinan, "Pastoral Letter (for First Sunday of Lent, February 19, 1961)," National Catholic Welfare Conference Office of the General Secretary, American Catholic History Research Center, Box 89, Folder 14, 3.

30. Shelley, *Paul J. Hallinan*, 125.

31. Untitled document (September 20, 1962), Diocese of Charleston Archives, Fr. William C. Burns Subject Files, Box 14, Folder: Vicar General 1962–1963 and 1965–1969.

32. Press release (September 19, 1962), *WCB*, Box 14, Folder: Vicar General 1962–1963 and 1965–1969. It may be of some interest to note that Msgr. Murphy, who joined Joseph as co-vicar general

in 1962, was the pastor of St. Peter's in Columbia who had urged Joseph into the priesthood.

33. Joseph L. Bernardin, "Foreword," in *Vatican II: By Those Who Were There*, Alberic Stacpoole, ed., (London: G. Chapman, 1986), xi.

34. Sam Miglarese interview with author, March 7, 2015, Hampton, SC.

35. Joseph L. Bernardin, "Diocese of Charleston: 1958–1962," 2.

36. Paul J. Hallinan, "The Renewal of the Liturgy," in *Days of Hope and Promise: The Writings and Speeches of Paul J. Hallinan, Archbishop of Atlanta*, Vincent A. Yzermans, ed., (Collegeville, MN: Liturgical Press, 1973), 63. Five decades later, Massimo Faggioli argued that liturgical renewal provides the interpretive key necessary to understand the Second Vatican Council, in *True Reform: Liturgy and Ecclesiololgy in* Sacrosanctum Concilium (Collegeville, MN: Liturgical Press, 2012).

37. "Change in the Catholic Church: Threat or Challenge?" *JLB*, Speeches & Talks, Folder "Talks—1968," 8.

38. Nancy Frazier, "Cardinal Bernardin Wants to Be No Different than Archbishop Bernardin," *The Catholic Banner* 15:6 (February 10, 1983): 1.

39. "To: Council of Churches—Beaufort, S.C." (1965?), *JLB*, Speeches & Talks, Folder "Talks—1965 & Prior," 3.

40. Michael Hirsley, "Journey to Rome Trained a Bishop," *Chicago Tribune* (April 26, 1991), 3.

41. Untitled installation homily (December 1972), *JLB*, Joseph Louis Bernardin Subject Files: "Talks, Homilies, Installation Festivities—Dec. 1972," 1.

Chapter Two:
The Youngest Bishop in America (1966–72)—
pages 24–48

1. Thomas J. Shelley, *Paul J. Hallinan: First Archbishop of Atlanta* (Wilmington, DE: Michael Glazier, Inc., 1989), 85.

2. Joseph L. Bernardin, interview by Kathi Stearns, March 1, 1996, Archdiocese of Atlanta Office of Archives & Records, Atlanta, GA.

3. Bishop James P. Shannon, *Our Sunday Visitor* (April 21, 1968), 14. Cited in John Tracy Ellis, "Archbishop Hallinan: In Memoriam," *Thought* 43:4 (Winter 1968), 539.

4. John Tracy Ellis, "A Tribute: '. . . With Prudence, With Courage, With Determination,'" in *Days of Hope and Promise: The Writings and Speeches of Paul J. Hallinan, Archbishop of Atlanta*, Vincent A. Yzermans, ed., (Collegeville, MN: Liturgical Press, 1973), v.

5. "Homily for the Funeral of Archbishop Paul J. Hallinan," *BJB*, Box 1, Folder 3.

6. Joseph L. Bernardin, "My Two Years in Atlanta," *Georgia Bulletin* (March 19, 1981), 3.

7. "Talk for Mass of Reception—Atlanta, May 4, 1966," *BJB*, Box 1, Folder 3, 1.

8. Ibid., 1

9. Ibid., 5.

10. "First Synod: Lay Congress Will Provide Prior Views," *Georgia Bulletin* (September 9, 1965).

11. See Shelley, *Paul J. Hallinan*, 260–61ff.

12. Paul J. Hallinan to priests (November 9, 1966), Archdiocese of Atlanta Archives, cited at Shelley, *Paul J. Hallinan*, 261

13. Bernardin, "My Two Years in Atlanta," 3.

14. Joseph L. Bernardin, "Homily: Mass Commemorating the 25th Anniversary of Episcopal Ordination" (April 28, 1991), in *Selected Works of Joseph Cardinal Bernardin, Volume One: Homilies and Teaching Documents*, Alphonse P. Spilly, CPPS, ed., (Collegeville, MN: Liturgical Press, 2000), 521.

15. NC News Service, "Bishop Says Liturgy Has Not Been Truly Effective," release issued by the Press Department, U.S. Catholic Conference (26 April 1967), *BJB*, Box 1, Folder 3, 1.

16. Joseph L. Bernardin, *"Interventus in Scriptis"* (October 11, 1974) in Archives of the University of Notre Dame, John F. Dearden Collection, CDRD 10/11, Folder "Synod of Bishops, 1974," 1.

17. Edward B. Fiske, "War and the Clergy," *New York Times* (February 15, 1966), 2.

18. Paul J. Hallinan and Joseph L. Bernardin, "War and Peace: A Pastoral Letter to the Archdiocese of Atlanta, October 1966," in John

Tracy Ellis, ed., *Documents of American Catholic History*, vol. 2 1866–1966 (Wilmington, DE: Michael Glazier, 1987), 696–702ff.

19. Untitled statement dated August, 1966, *BJB*, Box 1, Folder 3.

20. Paul J. Hallinan, typescript draft of manuscript for *Continuum* (October 21, 1964), in Archdiocese of Atlanta Office of Archives and Records, Archbishop Paul J. Hallinan Collection, Series 3, Folder 4.

21. Floyd Anderson, "Bishop Bernardin Gives Views on New Post," NC News Service release (April 13, 1968), *BJB*, Box 1, Folder 4.

22. *Georgia Bulletin*, March 18, 1965, cited in: Shelley, *Paul J. Hallinan*, 231.

23. See Andrew S. Moore, "Christian Unity, Lay Authority, and the People of God," in *Empowering the People of God: Catholic Action before and after Vatican II*, Jeremy Bonner, Mary Beth Fraser Connolly, and Christopher Denny, eds., (New York: Fordham University Press, 2014), 287–88. That African American parish, Our Lady of Lourdes, remains vibrantly open and identifies itself as "The Mother Church of African American Catholics in the Archdiocese of Atlanta." For a thoughtful analysis of a similar paradox on the road to integration, see the challenges posed to historically black colleges ("HBCs") in Jean L. Preer, *Lawyers vs. Educators: Black Colleges and Desegregation in Public Higher Education* (Westport, CT: Greenwood, 1982).

24. Program for "Votive Mass for Peace" (June 21, 1968), *BJB*, Box 1, Folder 1.

25. Religious News Service, "Archdiocese Will Probe Texts for Possible Anti-Semitism" (November 10, 1966), *BJB*, Box 1, Folder 3.

26. Pastoral Letter "The Church and Change . . . In the Age of Renewal" (Lent 1965), *PJH*, Box 3, Folder 14.

27. Shelley, *Paul J. Hallinan*, 288.

28. Ibid., 289.

29. Paul J. Hallinan to John F. Dearden (undated), *PJH*, Box 6, Folder 12.

30. "Homily for the Funeral of Archbishop Paul J. Hallinan" (April 1, 1968), *BJB*, Box 1, Folder 3.

31. Floyd Anderson (NC News Service), "Bishop Bernardin Gives Views on New Post" (April 13, 1968), *BJB*, Box 1, Folder 5.

32. Joseph L. Bernardin to Very Rev. Christopher Huntington (April 14, 1968), *BJB*, Box 1, Folder 5.

33. Memorandum to Joseph L. Bernardin from Father Edwin B. Neill (undated, marked "Aug. 1968"), in American Catholic History Research Center, NCCB Collection, Box 140, Folder "Ad Hoc Committee on Statutes: 1966–1968."

34. Joseph L. Bernardin to John F. Deardan (May 22, 1969), *NCCB*, Box 140, Folder "Ad Hoc Committee on Statutes: 1969."

35. Thomas J. Reese, *A Flock of Shepherds: The National Conference of Catholic Bishops* (Kansas City, MO: Sheed & Ward, 1982), 83.

36. Ibid., 83.

37. "Homily: Funeral Mass for John Cardinal Dearden," Cathedral of the Blessed Sacrament, Detroit, MI (August 5, 1988), *SW1*, 559.

38. Ibid., 558.

39. Eugene Kennedy, *Bernardin: Life to the Full* (Chicago: Bonus Books, 1997), 81.

40. Edward B. Fiske, "Most U.S. Priests Found to Oppose Birth Control Ban," *New York Times* (April 15, 1971), 31.

41. Lynne Langley, "Assistant Gets New Duties," *News & Courier* (August 29, 1982), 14F, in Diocese of Charleston Office of Archives and Record Management, Office of the Bishop Records, Box 59, Folder 5.

42. "Homily: Mass Commemorating the 25th Anniversary of Episcopal Ordination," Holy Name Cathedral, Chicago, IL (April 28, 1991), *SW1*, 521.

Chapter Three:
From Cautious Bureaucrat to Pastor (1972–82)—pages 49–72

1. Thomas Nolker interview with author via telephone, August 10, 2015.

2. Bruce Buursma, "New Archbishop Notes Spiritual Hunger Here," *Chicago Tribune* (August 24, 1982), 8, in Caroliniana Library (Columbia), Joseph Louis Bernardin Collection, Box 6, Folder 11.

3. Roger Antonio Fortin, *Faith and Action: A History of the Catholic Archdiocese of Cincinnati, 1821–1896* (Columbus: Ohio State University Press, 2002), 395–402.

4. Joseph L. Bernardin, "Catholic Education Address," at the Ursuline Center, Cincinnati, OH (April 4, 1973), in Archdiocese of

Chicago Joseph Cardinal Bernardin Archive and Records Center, Joseph Cardinal Bernardin Addresses and Talks Collection.

5. Joseph L. Bernardin, "Talk for the Dedication of Chaminade-Julienne High School," Dayton, OH (October 14, 1973), *JLB* Addresses & Talks Collection.

6. Bernardin, "Catholic Education Address."

7. Joseph L. Bernardin, "Archbishop Bernardin's Remarks Pastoral Council Meeting," Cincinnati, OH (January 28, 1973), *JLB*, Addresses & Talks Collection.

8. Alphonse P. Spilly, CPPS, interview with author, June 1, 2015, San Antonio, TX.

9. Joseph L. Bernardin, "Homily for Mass Observing Second Anniversary of the Supreme Court Abortion Decision," Cathedral of Saint Peter in Chains, Cincinnati, OH (January 22, 1975), *JLB*, Addresses & Talks Collection.

10. Joseph L. Bernardin, "Homily for Mass Commemorating Third Anniversary of the Supreme Court's Abortion Decision," Cathedral of St. Peter in Chains, Cincinnati, OH (January 22, 1976), *JLB*, Addresses & Talks Collection.

11. Joseph L. Bernardin, "The Social Teachings of the Church: A Call to Unity," address to the Serra International Convention, Philadelphia, PA (June 25, 1975), *JLB*, Addresses & Talks Collection.

12. James S. Rausch, "Memorandum: Developments Subsequent to the Andrew Young Breakfast," The American Catholic History Research Center, Washington, DC, NCCB Collection, Box 63, Folder "Ad Hoc Committee on Pro-Life Activities: Jul.-Sept., 1976."

13. John F. Dearden, "The Church's Bicentennial Program: Potential for Coalition Building," *NCCB*, Box 119, Folder, "Ad Hoc Committee on the Bicentennial 1976—Jan.-Jun."

14. Joseph L. Bernardin, "Statement Relative to the 'Call to Action' Conference," Detroit, MI (October 26, 1976), *JLB*, Addresses & Talks Collection.

15. John F. Dearden, "Report to the NCCB by the *ad hoc* Committee for the Bicentennial" (November 1, 1976), in Archives of the Archdiocese of Detroit, John F. Dearden Collection, Box 5, Folder 14.

16. Joseph L. Bernardin to John F. Dearden (April 20, 1977), *JCD*, Box 5, Folder 15.

17. Eugene Kennedy, *My Brother Joseph: The Spirit of a Cardinal and the Story of a Friendship* (New York: St. Martin's Press, 1997), 138.

18. Larry Carney, "Cardinal 'Iron John' Dearden: The 'Prince' Who Became a Servant," *Catholic New Times* 28:4 (February 29, 2004), 16.

19. Bishop Ken Untener, *The Practical Prophet: Pastoral Writings* (Mahwah, NJ: Paulist Press, 2007), 273.

20. Quoted at Ibid., 272.

21. Joseph L. Bernardin, "Homily on St. Francis (for Assisi)" (May 1975), *JLB*, Addresses & Talks Collection.

22. Carolyn Croke, executive director for the Holy Name Province, to author (July 9, 2015).

23. Michael Place to author (July 13, 2015). Also Alphonse Spilly.

24. Bernardin, "Homily on St. Francis (for Assisi)."

25. Joseph L. Bernardin, "Institute of Spirituality; Talk No.1: "Personal Prayer – Why?" (version one), St. Paul, MN (June 11, 1974), *JLB*, Addresses & Talks Collection.

26. Joseph L. Bernardin, "Institute of Spirituality; Talk No. 2: "Personal Prayer – How?" St. Paul, MN (June 11, 1974), *JLB*, Addresses & Talks Collection.

27. Ibid.

28. Joseph L. Bernardin, "'Resting' Retreat Conference – IV," *JLB*, Addresses & Talks Collection.

29. Joseph L. Bernardin, "'Feeding' Retreat Conference – III," *JLB*, Addresses & Talks Collection.

30. Ibid.

31. Bernardin, "Institute of Spirituality; Talk No.1: "Personal Prayer—Why?" (version one).

32. Ibid.

33. Joseph L. Bernardin, "Christ Lives in Me," in *Selected Works of Joseph Cardinal Bernardin, Volume One: Homilies and Teaching Documents*, Alphonse P. Spilly, CPPS, ed., (Collegeville, MN: Liturgical Press, 2000), 129.

34. Bernardin, "Institute of Spirituality; Talk No.1: "Personal Prayer—Why?" (version one).

35. Joseph L. Bernardin, "Freedom Today" (February 21, 1978), *JLB*, Addresses & Talks Collection.

36. Joseph L. Bernardin, "Homily for Separated and Divorced Catholics," St. Rita Parish, Dayton, OH (January 12, 1979), *JLB*, Addresses & Talks Collection.

37. Joseph L. Bernardin, "Talk for the Brotherhood Service," Isaac M. Wise Temple, Cincinnati, OH (February 15, 1974), *JLB*, Addresses & Talks Collection.

Chapter Four:
"I Am Joseph, Your Brother" (1982–93)—
pages 73–93

1. Edward R. Kantowicz, "The Beginning and the End of an Era: George William Mundelein and John Patrick Cody in Chicago," in *Catholicism, Chicago Style* (Chicago: Loyola University Press, 1993), 155.

2. Joseph L. Bernardin, "Homily: 'I Am Joseph, Your Brother,'" Holy Name Cathedral, Chicago, IL (August 24, 1982), in *Selected Works of Joseph Cardinal Bernardin, Volume One: Homilies and Teaching Documents*, Alphonse P. Spilly, CPPS, ed., (Collegeville, MN: Liturgical Press, 2000), 283.

3. Joseph L. Bernardin, "Homily for the Farewell Masses," (August 1982), in Archdiocese of Chicago Joseph Cardinal Bernardin Archive and Records Center, Joseph Cardinal Bernardin Addresses & Talks Collection.

4. Bernardin, "Homily: I Am Joseph, Your Brother," 282.

5. Joseph L. Bernardin, "Our Communion, Our Peace, Our Promise: Pastoral Letter on the Liturgy" (February 1984), *SW1*, 521.

6. Ibid., 17, 23.

7. Eugene Kennedy, *Bernardin: Life to the Full* (Chicago: Bonus Books, 1997), 204.

8. Quoted in Thomas J. Reese, SJ, *A Flock of Shepherds: The National Conference of Catholic Bishops* (Kansas City, MO: Sheed & Ward, 1992), 120.

9. Mary McGrory, "WAR," *Washington Post* (November 18, 1982).

10. William P. Clark, "Text of Administration's Letter to U.S. Catholic Bishops on Nuclear Policies," *New York Times* (November 17, 1982), B4.

11. Joseph L. Bernardin, "Address: 'A Consistent Ethic of Life: An American-Catholic Dialogue,' " Fordham University, New York, NY (December 6, 1983), in *Selected Works of Joseph Cardinal Bernardin, Volume Two: Church and Society*, Alphonse P. Spilly, CPPS, ed., (Collegeville, MN: Liturgical Press, 2000), 81, 82.

12. Ibid., 86.

13. Ibid., 86.

14. Quoted at Margaret Ross Sammon, "The Politics of the U.S. Catholic Bishops: The Centrality of Abortion," in *Catholics and Politics: The Dynamic Tension between Faith and Power*, Kristin E. Heyer, Mark J. Rozell, and Michael E. Genovese, eds., (Washington, DC: Georgetown University Press, 2008), 19.

15. Ibid., 187, 19.

16. Joseph L. Bernardin, "The Consistent Ethic of Life: Its Theological Foundation, Its Ethical Logic, and Its Political Consequences," Seattle University, Seattle, WA (March 2, 1986), *SW2*, 110–111.

17. John Canary interview with author, May 29, 2015, Chicago, IL.

18. "Chicago Prelate Is Accused of Sex Abuse and Denies It," *New York Times* (November 13, 1993), 12.

19. Thomas Nolker interview with author via telephone, August 10, 2015.

20. John Canary, interview.

21. Ibid.

22. Joseph L. Bernardin, "Homily: Diamond Jubilee of Theological College," The Catholic University of America, Washington, DC (October 1, 1992), *JLB*, Addresses & Talks Collection.

23. Jerry Falwell had said that, "AIDS is not just God's punishment for homosexuals, it is God's punishment for the society that tolerates homosexuals," and Billy Graham allowed that, "AIDS may be a judgment of God upon us." See Hans Johnson and William Eskridge, "The Legacy of Falwell's Bully Pulpit," *Washington Post* (May 19, 2007); and Anthony M. Petro, *After the Wrath of God: AIDS, Sexuality, and American Religion* (New York: Oxford University Press, 2015), 28. In fairness to Rev. Graham, he retracted that statement in 1993, seven years after he made it.

24. Joseph L. Bernardin, "Statement Regarding Advertising of Condoms" (February 19, 1987), *JLB*, Addresses & Talks Collection.

25. Joseph L. Bernardin, "A Challenge and a Responsibility: A Pastoral Statement on the Church's Response to the AIDS Crisis" (October 24, 1986), *SW1*, 188.

26. Place, interview.

27. Kenneth Velo interview with author, May 29, 2015, Chicago, IL.

28. L. Scott Donahue interview with author, December 27, 2014, Chicago, IL.

29. Ibid.

30. Velo, interview, May 29, 2015.

Chapter Five:
A Challenge and Peace (1993–96)—pages 94–114

1. Alphonse Spilly, CPPS, interview with author, June 1, 2015. San Antonio, TX. Father Spilly remembered Joseph's words recounting the meeting with Pope John Paul.

2. Thomas C. Fox and Dawn Gibeau, "Accusers counsel a critic of Cardinal Bernardin," *National Catholic Reporter* 30:6 (December 3, 1993), 6.

3. Gustav Niebuhr, "Bernardin Memoir Suggests Priest Urged Accuser," *New York Times* (February 1, 1997).

4. In *The Gift of Peace*, Joseph himself tells us that "It became clear to me that certain critics of mine had played a role in urging Steven Cook to take on the role of plaintiff against me" (32).

5. Joseph L. Bernardin, *The Gift of Peace* (Chicago: Loyola University Press, 1997), 16–17.

6. Joseph L. Bernardin, "Address: The Priests of the Archdiocese," Niles College Seminary, Niles, IL (November 19, 1993), in Archdiocese of Chicago Joseph Cardinal Bernardin Archive and Records Center, Joseph Cardinal Bernardin Addresses & Talks Collection.

7. L. Scott Donahue interview with author, December 27, 2014, Chicago, IL.

8. Kenneth Velo interview with author, May 29, 2015, Chicago, IL.

9. Donahue, interview.

10. Joseph L. Bernardin, "Address: 'Anti-Semitism: The Historical Legacy and the Continuing Challenge for Christians," in *Selected Works of Joseph Cardinal Bernardin, Volume Two: Church and So-*

ciety, Alphonse P. Spilly, CPPS, ed., (Collegeville, MN: Liturgical Press, 2000), 292.

11. Ibid., 296.

12. Ibid., 297.

13. Ibid., 298.

14. Bob Secter and Tara Gruzen, "Clergy of Many Faiths Remember Friend Who Built Bridges to Them," *Chicago Tribune* (November 20, 1996).

15. Bernardin, *The Gift of Peace*, 39.

16. Ibid., 39–40.

17. Velo interview, May 29, 2015.

18. Velo interview, March 18, 2015.

19. Bernardin, *Gift of Peace*, 127–28.

20. Henri Nouwen, *Our Greatest Gift: A Meditation on Dying and Caring* (New York: HarperCollins, 1995), 100.

21. Velo, interview, March 18, 2015.

22. Joseph L. Bernardin, "Remarks: Catholic Common Ground News Conference," Chicago, IL (August 12, 1996), *SW2*, 311.

23. Ibid., 311–12.

24. Gustav Niebuhr, "Cardinal Opposed in Effort to Find Common Ground," *New York Times* (August 24, 1996).

25. Velo, interview, March 18, 2015.

26. Michael Place interview with author, May 30, 2015, Michigan City, IN.

27. Velo, interview, March 18, 2015.

28. Ibid.

Conclusion—pages 115–17

1. Joseph L. Bernardin, "Christ Lives in Me: A Pastoral Reflection on Jesus and His Meaning for Christian Life," in *Selected Works of Joseph Cardinal Bernardin: Volume 2, Church and Society,* Alphonse P. Spilly, CPPS, ed., (Collegeville, MN: Liturgical Press, 2000), 112.

2. Ibid., 112.

Bibliography

Archival Collections

Administration of Cemeteries 1952–1959 Collection. Diocese of Charleston Archive.

Archbishop Paul J. Hallinan Collection. Archdiocese of Atlanta Office of Archives and Records.

Bishop Joseph L. Bernardin Collection. Archdiocese of Atlanta Office of Archives and Records.

Fr. William C. Burns Subject Files. Diocese of Charleston Archive.

John Cardinal Dearden Collection. Archdiocese of Detroit Archives.

John F. Dearden Papers. University of Notre Dame Archives.

Joseph Louis Bernardin Collection. Archdiocese of Chicago Joseph Cardinal Bernardin Archives and Records Center.

Joseph Louis Bernardin Collection. Caroliniana Library.

National Catholic Welfare Conference Office of the General Secretary Collection. American Catholic History Research Center.

NCCB Collection. American Catholic History Research Center.

Office of the Bishop Records. Diocese of Charleston Archive.

Priest Subject Files. Diocese of Charleston Archives.

Books

Anderson, R. Bentley. *Black, White, and Catholic: New Orleans Interracialism, 1947–1956.* Nashville: Vanderbilt University Press, 2005.

Bernardin, Joseph L. *The Gift of Peace*. Chicago: Loyola Press, 1997.

Ellis, John Tracy, ed., *Documents of American Catholic History*. 2 vols. Wilmington, DE: Michael Glazier, Inc., 1987.

Fortin, Roger Antonio. *Faith and Action: A History of the Catholic Archdiocese of Cincinnati, 1821–1896*. Columbus, OH: Ohio State University Press, 2002.

Kantowicz, Edward R. "The Beginning and the End of an Era: George William Mundelein and John Patrick Cody in Chicago." In *Catholicism, Chicago Style*. Chicago: Loyola University Press, 1993.

Kennedy, Eugene. *My Brother Joseph: The Spirit of a Cardinal and the Story of a Friendship*. New York: St. Martin's Press, 1997.

_____. *Bernardin: Life to the Full*. Chicago: Bonus Books, 1997.

Moore, Andrew S. "Christian Unity, Lay Authority, and the People of God." In *Empowering the People of God: Catholic Action before and after Vatican II*. New York: Fordham University Press, 2014.

Nouwen, Henri. *Our Greatest Gift: A Meditation on Dying and Caring*. New York: HarperCollins, 1995.

Reese, Thomas J. *A Flock of Shepherds: The National Conference of Catholic Bishops*. Kansas City, MO: Sheed & Ward, 1982.

Sammon, Margaret Ross. "The Politics of the U.S. Bishops: The Centrality of Abortion." In *Catholics and Politics: The Dynamic Tension between Faith and Power*. Washington, DC: Georgetown University Press, 2008.

Shelley, Thomas J. *Paul J. Hallinan: First Archbishop of Atlanta*. Wilmington, DE: Michael Glazier, Inc., 1989.

Spilly, Alphonse P., ed. *Selected Works of Joseph Cardinal Bernardin*. 2 vols. Collegeville, MN: Liturgical Press, 2000.

Stacpoole, Alberic, ed. *Vatican II: By Those Who Were There*. London: G. Chapman, 1986.

Untener, Ken. *The Practical Prophet: Pastoral Writings*. Mahwah, NJ: Paulist Press, 2007.

Yzermans, Vincent A., ed. *Days of Hope and Promise: The Writings and Speeches of Paul J. Hallinan.* Collegeville, MN: Liturgical Press, 1973.

Periodicals

Bernardin, Joseph L. "My Two Years in Atlanta." *The Georgia Bulletin* (March 19, 1981).

Carney, Larry. "Cardinal 'Iron John' Dearden: The 'Prince Who Became a Servant.'" *Catholic New Times* 28:4 (February 29, 2004).

Clark, William P. "Text of Administration's Letter to U.S. Catholic Bishops on Nuclear Policies." *New York Times* (November 17, 1982): B4.

Ellis, John Tracy. "Archbishop Hallinan: In Memoriam." *Thought* 43:4 (Winter 1968).

Falsani, Cathleen. "Beloved Cousin Joe Is Missed Already." *Chicago Tribune* (November 18, 1996).

Fiske, Edward B. "Most U.S. Priests Found to Oppose Birth Control Ban." *New York Times* (April 15, 1971).

Fox, Thomas C. and Dawn Gibeau. "Accusers counsel a critic of Cardinal Bernardin." *National Catholic Reporter* 30:6 (December 3, 1993): 6.

Frazier, Nancy. "Cardinal Bernardin Wants to Be No Different than Archbishop Bernardin." *The Catholic Banner* 15:6 (February 10, 1983): 1.

Georgia Bulletin. "First Synod: Lay Congress Will Provide Prior Views." (September 9, 1965).

Gratteau, Hanke. "Bernardin Clan's Trip Here a Thrill." *Chicago Sun-Times* (August 25, 1982): 1.

Hirsley, Michael. "Journey to Rome Trained a Bishop." *Chicago Tribune* (April 26, 1991).

McGrory, Mary. "WAR." *Washington Post* (November 18, 1982).

McLean, Thomas. "Cardinal Bernardin." *The State* (January 30, 1983): 5B.

New York Times. "Cardinal Opposed in Effort to Find Common Ground." (August 24, 1996).

———. "Chicago Prelate Is Accused of Sex Abuse and Denies It." (November 13, 1993): 12.

———. "War and the Clergy." (February 15, 1966).

Niebuhr, Gustav. "Bernardin Memoir Suggests Priest Urged Accuser." *New York Times* (February 1, 1997).

Secter, Bob, and Tara Gruzen. "Clergy of Many Faiths Remember Friend Who Built Bridges to Them." *Chicago Tribune* (November 20, 1996).

Interviews

While not all of these subject interviews generated quotations used in this book, all of these conversations immeasurably enriched the author's understanding of Joseph Bernardin. Each conversation addressed a different aspect of Bernardin's life, and all of them were essential.

Bernardin, Libby. Interview by author. April 28, 2015. Columbia, SC.

Cameli, Rev. Louis J. Interview by author. August 4, 2015. Chicago, IL.

Canary, Msgr. John. Interview by author. May 29, 2015. Chicago, IL.

Donahue, Rev. L. Scott. Interview by author. December 27, 2014. Chicago, IL.

Gregory, Most Rev. Wilton. Interview by author. April 30, 2015. Smyrna, GA.

McGinty, Joan. Interview by author. March 9, 2015. Aiken, SC.

Miglarese, Pastor Sam. Interview by author. March 7, 2015. Hampton, SC.

Nolker, Rev. Thomas. Interview by author. August 10, 2015. Via telephone from Cincinnati, OH.

Orf, Anita Bernardin. Interview by author. October 28, 2014. Columbia, SC.

Place, Rev. Michael. Interview by author. May 30, 2015. Michigan City, IN.

Rohr, Rev. Richard, OFM. Interview by author. July 13, 2015. Via email from Albuquerque, NM.

Spilly, Rev. Alphonse, CPPS. Interview by author. June 1, 2015. San Antonio, TX.

Velo, Msgr. Kenneth. Interview by author. March 18, 2015. Chicago, IL.

_____. Interview by author. May 29, 2015. Chicago, IL.

Index